Diversity and the Study of Antiquity in Higher Education

This volume explores how the study of antiquity can be made relevant and inclusive for a diverse range of twenty-first-century students by bringing together perspectives from colleagues working in higher education at different career stages, roles, and from different backgrounds in the US, UK, and Greece.

This collection of chapters addresses issues related to inclusive practice and diversity in Classics Higher Education, especially in the US and the UK. Recent debates within the discipline have highlighted inequality of access to traditional classical education, and a growing number of initiatives and projects have begun to address the range of sources and topics that form part of a modern classical education. The discipline is wide-ranging, including study of ancient Greek and Latin language and literature (the traditional core of Classics), as well as opportunities to study the ancient history, philosophy, religion, mythology, material culture, and archaeology of the Greco-Roman period. Significant progress has been made over recent years in incorporating the study of gender and sexuality within classical degree programmes, and increasingly programmes are being enriched through broadening the geographical reach of topics on the curriculum beyond Europe. More care is also being taken over selection of scholarly reading to represent more fully the range of voices contributing to the discipline. But more work remains to be done.

Diversity and the Study of Antiquity in Higher Education is of interest to anyone teaching Classics, especially in the US and UK, as well as scholars and researchers in the field who are interested in issues of diversity.

Daniel Libatique is Vincent J. Rosivach Professor of Classical Studies at Fairfield University, USA.

Fiona McHardy is Professor of Classics at University of Roehampton, UK.

Classics In and Out of the Academy: Classical Pedagogy in the Twenty-First Century
Series editors – Fiona McHardy and Nancy Rabinowitz

This series of short volumes explores the ways in which the study of antiquity can enrich the lives of diverse populations in the twenty-first century. The series covers two distinct, but interrelated topics: 1) ways in which classicists can engage new audiences within the profession by embedding inclusivity and diversity in school and university teaching practices, curricula, and assessments, and 2) the relevance of Classics to learners from the most marginalized social strata (e.g. the incarcerated, refugees, those suffering from mental illness).

Classics and Prison Education in the US
Edited by Emilio Capettini and Nancy Sorkin Rabinowitz

Classics at Primary School
A Tool for Social Justice
Evelien Bracke

Expanding Classics
Practitioner Perspectives from Museums and Schools
Edited by Arlene Holmes-Henderson

Diversity and the Study of Antiquity in Higher Education
Perspectives from North America and Europe
Edited by Daniel Libatique and Fiona McHardy

Diversity and the Study of Antiquity in Higher Education
Perspectives from North America and Europe

Edited by
Daniel Libatique and
Fiona McHardy

LONDON AND NEW YORK

First published 2023
by Routledge
4 Park Square, Milton Park, Abingdon, Oxon OX14 4RN

and by Routledge
605 Third Avenue, New York, NY 10158

Routledge is an imprint of the Taylor & Francis Group, an informa business

© 2023 selection and editorial matter, Daniel Libatique and Fiona McHardy; individual chapters, the contributors

The right of Daniel Libatique and Fiona McHardy to be identified as the authors of the editorial material, and of the authors for their individual chapters, has been asserted in accordance with sections 77 and 78 of the Copyright, Designs and Patents Act 1988.

All rights reserved. No part of this book may be reprinted or reproduced or utilised in any form or by any electronic, mechanical, or other means, now known or hereafter invented, including photocopying and recording, or in any information storage or retrieval system, without permission in writing from the publishers.

Trademark notice: Product or corporate names may be trademarks or registered trademarks, and are used only for identification and explanation without intent to infringe.

British Library Cataloguing-in-Publication Data
A catalogue record for this book is available from the British Library

Library of Congress Cataloging-in-Publication Data
Names: Libatique, Daniel, editor. | McHardy, Fiona, editor.
Title: Diversity and the study of antiquity in higher education : perspectives from North America and Europe / edited by Daniel Libatique and Fiona McHardy.
Description: Abingdon, Oxon ; New York, NY : Routledge, 2023. | Series: Classics in and out of the academy | Includes bibliographical references and index.
Identifiers: LCCN 2022057138 (print) | LCCN 2022057139 (ebook) | ISBN 9781032235127 (hardback) | ISBN 9781032235134 (paperback) | ISBN 9781003278016 (ebook)
Subjects: LCSH: Classical literature--Study and teaching (Higher)--North America. | Classical literature--Study and teaching (Higher)--Europe. | Classical languages--Study and teaching (Higher)--North America. | Classical languages--Study and teaching (Higher)--Europe. | Multicultural education--North America. | Multicultural education--Europe.
Classification: LCC PA3013 .D58 2023 (print) | LCC PA3013 (ebook) | DDC 880.071/1--dc23/eng/20230313
LC record available at https://lccn.loc.gov/2022057138
LC ebook record available at https://lccn.loc.gov/2022057139

ISBN: 978-1-032-23512-7 (hbk)
ISBN: 978-1-032-23513-4 (pbk)
ISBN: 978-1-003-27801-6 (ebk)

DOI: 10.4324/9781003278016

Typeset in Times New Roman
by KnowledgeWorks Global Ltd.

Contents

List of Contributors   vii

Introduction: Diversity and the Study of Antiquity in Higher Education   1
DANIEL LIBATIQUE AND FIONA McHARDY

1 **Affectionate Ties: The Discipline of the Classics and the College or University Mission**   9
PATRICE RANKINE

2 **Digging Deeper: Toward a More Inclusive Archaeology of the Ancient Mediterranean**   25
NADHIRA HILL

3 **'Classics Beyond Whiteness': Race and Antiracism in Departmental Curriculum**   36
T. H. M. GELLAR-GOAD AND CAITLIN HINES

4 **Race, Roman Law Courts, and the Colonized Subject: Teaching Cicero's *Pro Fonteio***   47
DENISE EILEEN McCOSKEY

5 **A Classical Studies Pedagogy for the Future: An Introspective Look**   61
ELENI BOZIA

Contents

6 **Looking Up, Looking Online: Gender, Representation, and Bias in Classics**   72
VICTORIA LEONARD

7 **'Biting the Hand that Feeds You?' Responding to Racialisation in UK Classics**   88
SAMUEL AGBAMU

8 **Teaching Visual/Material Culture and Museums in Terms of Disability Access**   100
ELLEN ADAMS

9 **'Reaching Out with Eurydice': The Myth and Voice Initiative**   110
EFROSSINI SPENTZOU

10 **Inclusive Classics and Pedagogy: Teachers, Academics, and Students in Conversation**   121
BARBARA GOFF AND ALEXIA PETSALIS-DIOMIDIS

11 **Embedding Diversity in Classics Teachers' Training: A Case Study at a Greek University**   131
MARISA FOUNTOPOULOU AND EFFROSYNI KOSTARA

Index   142

Contributors

Ellen Adams, Reader in Classical Archaeology and Liberal Arts, King's College London

Samuel Agbamu, Lecturer in Classics, University of Reading

Eleni Bozia, Associate Professor of Classics and Digital Humanities, University of Florida

Marisa Fountopoulou, Professor, Philosophy Pedagogy and Psychology, National and Kapodistrian University of Athens

T. H. M. Gellar-Goad, Associate Professor of Classics, Wake Forest University

Barbara Goff, Professor of Classics, University of Reading

Caitlin Hines, Assistant Professor of Classics, University of Cincinnati

Nadhira Hill, PhD Candidate, University of Michigan

Effrosyni Kostara, Adjunct Lecturer, Hellenic Open University and Research Associate at the Institute of Education Policy, Greece

Victoria Leonard, Fellow of the Royal Historical Society, Research Fellow at Centre for Arts, Memory and Communities, Coventry University, and Research Fellow at the Institute of Classical Studies, University of London

Denise Eileen McCoskey, Professor of Classics, University of Miami

Alexia Petsalis-Diomidis, Senior Lecturer in Classics, University of St. Andrews

Patrice Rankine, Professor of Classics, University of Chicago

Efrossini Spentzou, Reader in Latin Language and Literature, Royal Holloway, University of London

Introduction
Diversity and the Study of Antiquity in Higher Education

Daniel Libatique and Fiona McHardy

This volume had its origins in an event on 'Diversity and the Study of the Ancient World' held at the University of Roehampton in October 2017 where participants discussed teaching aspects of gender, sexuality, race, mental health, and disability in and beyond university classrooms, as well as the significance of diversity for the disciplines of Classics and Archaeology in the United Kingdom, Greece, and the United States.[1] Since then, contributors to this volume have organised or participated in a number of other related events including the 'Classics and Race: Research and Pedagogy' workshop at the University of St. Andrews in 2019, the panel on 'Addressing Issues of Social Justice in the Classroom' at the SCS conference in Washington in 2020, the 'Towards a more Inclusive Classics' workshop in 2020, and 'Towards a More Inclusive Classics II' international conference in 2021, the UK Classical Association's 'Inclusive Classics' panel in 2021, the Presidential Panel on 'Being Black in Classics' at CAMWS in 2021, the OIKOS 'Shared Antiquity' conference in the Netherlands in 2021, the panel on 'Race and Racism in the Roman World' at the UK Classical Association in 2022, and the Roundtable on 'Classics and "the Other"' at the University of Birmingham, UK in 2022. Contributors have also been involved in publishing important reports, chapters and articles on inclusivity and diversity within the discipline.[2] At the same time, numerous groups dedicated to supporting students and scholars from diverse backgrounds and to improving the discipline to make it more inclusive have begun to flourish.[3] The blossoming activity of these groups and increasing numbers of related publications and events is indicative of growing recognition within the profession of difficulties of inequality of access and barriers to success.

The present interest in appreciating, enhancing, and embedding diversity in higher education programmes and communities that study antiquity is mirrored in other educational settings and across society

DOI: 10.4324/9781003278016-1

more broadly. Despite the political, collective nature of society, in the sense that any given society is made up of people who bring different life experiences and diverse traits together to constitute the body politic, many people have experienced feelings of exclusion and alienation based on their identity.[4] Attempts to address these problems have resulted in a focus on improving 'diversity' which increasingly appears as a buzzword in job postings, institutional mission statements, political campaigns, and almost any aspect of modern society that one can imagine. This prevalence stems from the desire to address past and present failures to embrace diversity and the consequent oppression of substantial groups of people in UK and US society,[5] although this desire has simultaneously been met with resistance.[6]

Diversity as a concept rests on the perception of difference along any number of facets of identity: race, gender, physical and mental ability, religion, sexual orientation, economic status, class, and so on.[7] The concept itself is a value-neutral proposition: it is undeniable that such differences exist. Proponents of embracing diversity say that not only the acknowledgement but also the celebration of these differences create a body politic that is stronger for the multiple points of view and strengths that each individual member brings to the collective whole. However, when that acknowledgment or celebration of difference gives rise to a value judgment of perceived inferiority or superiority, we create polarities that situate some identities as 'normative' or 'ideal' and those that do not conform as 'non-normative,' 'deviant,' or even 'dangerous.' We concomitantly veer into undue idolatry or lionisation of those 'normative' identities on one end of the spectrum and blatant racism, sexism, xenophobia, or LGBTQ+-phobia against those who do not conform on the other. Diversity thus can become a measurement of how far a person strays from the 'norm' as a cause for disenfranchisement or even punishment.

The perception of diversity plays a large role in many current debates over law, education, politics, and indeed many other aspects of society in both US and European contexts. With regard to the former, one example will illustrate how diversity, or, rather, a failure to acknowledge the role diversity has played in systemic disenfranchisement, provides grounds for cultural reflection.

In the spring of 2022, the state of Florida rejected 54 out of 132 mathematics textbooks (41%) slated to be on the Florida Department of Education's K-12 adoption list.[8] According to state administrators, this rejection was due to the textbooks' inclusion of 'references to Critical Race Theory (CRT), inclusions of Common Core, and the unsolicited addition of Social Emotional Learning (SEL) in mathematics.'⁹ The review process appeared confusing and contradictory, with conservative activists turned textbook reviewers flagging any material that seemed to reference any kind of inequality or critical thinking, with terms like 'race,' 'developing grit,' or even 'wage gap' serving as grounds for rejection.[10]

The first topic, CRT, has become a rallying cry for conservatives seeking to demonise discussions of race and the systemic perpetuation of racism in and by social and political institutions. They ostensibly seek to prevent discussions from taking place in classrooms but by extension also those happening in culture more generally. Ron DeSantis, Florida's governor, at a bill-signing ceremony banning the teaching of CRT in K-12 schools, said, 'We are not gonna tell some kindergartener that they're an oppressor based on their race and what may have happened 100 or 200 years ago. And we're not gonna tell other kids that they're oppressed based on their race.'[11]

This framing deliberately obfuscates and misrepresents the major points of CRT, a theory based in legal studies that holds that race is a social construction and racism is fundamentally woven into social and political structures like education and the law.[12] The focus is on racist institutions, rather than any one individual's racist actions (though those may themselves be conditioned by the society and institutions around that individual): 'critical race theory states that U.S. social institutions (e.g., the criminal justice system, education system, labor market, housing market, and healthcare system) are laced with racism embedded in laws, regulations, rules, and procedures that lead to differential outcomes by race.'[13] Beginning in the 70s and 80s with the work of black legal scholars like Derrick Bell and Kimberlé Crenshaw, the framework argues that race has been used to disenfranchise individuals through the mechanisms that govern daily life, and it seeks to draw our attention to the ways in which racism affects our lives in both overt and more subtle ways.

Conservative objections to CRT being taught in grade schools and 'indoctrinating' children fail on two counts. First, by and large, CRT is not actually being taught at the K-12 level, though CRT-related concepts may inflect history or literature lessons: 'There is little to no evidence that critical race theory itself is being taught to K-12 public school students, though some ideas central to it, such as lingering consequences of slavery, have been.'[14] Second, acknowledging diversity and the value judgments attached to perceptions of difference shines a light on the inequality baked into the structures of power that govern society and politics. By rejecting the instruments by which people can be educated about these historical and ongoing injustices, politicians like DeSantis aim to rewrite the narrative in a manner flattering to those in hegemonic positions of power so that they can quash any claims as to that power's illegitimacy; as Crenshaw notes, the debate over CRT is not 'about a real difference in opinion, nor is it a debate that is winnable ... This is about a weapon they're using to hold on to power.'[15] They seek to homogenise a heterogenous, diverse population by claiming that all, regardless of race, are on an equal footing, and that the systemic injustices of the past no longer exist or have no repercussions in the present. Such a failure to reckon with objectively discriminatory structures that are based on or grew out of differences in race, gender, religion, and so on perpetuates inequality and deliberately misleads a population that needs to learn how to root out these systemic injustices.

These conversations about and conflicts regarding diversity relate to all aspects of social and political life, including higher education. As spaces that (generally) encourage the collocation of people from various walks of life, institutions of higher education are able not only to educate their students, staff, and faculty about diversity and its concomitant issues in classrooms and offices but also to embody diverse ideals in the very makeup of its community.

Diversity in the study of antiquity has meaning in both an ancient and a modern context. With regard to the former, much excellent work has been done in showing how ancient communities defined their identities in relation to one another, acknowledging (if not valuing) diversity in many contexts, including but not limited to race, ethnicity, geography, gender, sexuality, and physical and mental ability.[16] The peoples of the ancient Mediterranean world interacted with a variety of ideals, perspectives, and languages brought into conversation through the forces of trade, migration, and war, and their perceptions of and value judgments around difference led to culturally contingent debates and issues as loaded and essential to them as the discussions around concepts like CRT are to us in the modern day.

Recent debates within the discipline have highlighted inequality of access to traditional classical education and subsequently access to the profession.[17] A growing number of initiatives and projects have begun to address the range of sources and topics that form part of a modern classical education. Significant progress has been made recently in incorporating the study of gender and sexuality within classical degree programmes, and increasingly programmes are being enriched through broadening the geographical reach of topics on the curriculum beyond Europe.[18] More care is also being taken over selection of scholarly reading to represent more fully the range of voices contributing to the discipline, though issues persist with access to publication by scholars from diverse backgrounds.[19] Much more work remains to be done.

As practitioners within higher education settings, it is imperative that we acknowledge differences within society and consider how we can engage these differences to provide an inclusive environment where everyone can participate fully. An inclusive approach to learning and teaching in Classics can challenge students in ways that help them to succeed as students and as graduates. Recent years have seen universities prioritising projects to support inclusive learning and diversifying the offering. Because of different social contexts and individuals involved, there is no one way to do this work. The contributors to this volume identify a range of techniques and content that have worked in developing their courses in a variety of universities and put forward ideas for future progress.

This collection comprises two halves based on location (namely the US and the UK/Greece) and the issues relating to diversity in the study of antiquity specific to those regions. The chapters approach the study of the ancients with specific attention paid to the material, social, and political realities of the modern people who will engage in that study. The contributions cover a range that includes addressing teaching methods on specific courses (Gellar-Goad and Hines, McCoskey, Bozia, Fountopoulou, and Kostara), considering outreach and knowledge exchange between those in higher education and other related areas such as schools and museums (Adams, Spentzou), and considering diversity in the discipline more broadly (Rankine, Hill, Leonard, Agbamu, Goff, and Petsalis-Diomidis). The breadth of topics covered by our contributors addresses diversity in various aspects of academic life, from race and ethnicity to disability to gender, and our contributors themselves bring valuable life experiences and innovative approaches to diversity in the study of antiquity. It is hoped that this volume will inspire ongoing discussions and developments in this burgeoning field.

Notes

1 See Kostara's (2018) report on the event.
2 Rankine (2019), (2020); Leonard and Lovatt (2020); Adams (2021); McCoskey (2022). Cf. also Leonard et al. (2016).
3 These include, but are not limited to, the Sportula, London Classicists of Colour, The Mountaintop Coalition, Asterion, the Network for Working Class Classicists.
4 Re. Classics, see, e.g., Blouin (2017) on the SCS conference in Toronto.
5 See Hakkola and Ropers-Huilman (2018) on difficulties of increasing diversity in admissions to Higher Education in the US.
6 See, e.g., Pandey (2021) where Prof. Katharina Wesselmann talks about fear among conservative German Classicists concerning 'cancel culture.'

7 See Pineda and Mishra (2022) for the evolution of the term and what it covers over time. They trace the roots of diversity as a concept in the US civil rights movements and its subsequent embedding in UK and European higher education in the 2000s. They note that the term is not equally valorised across the world and there is a lack of focus on the ideal of diversity in higher education in the global south.
8 See https://www.fldoe.org/core/fileparse.php/5574/urlt/2122MathAdopted Materials.pdf
9 See https://www.fldoe.org/newsroom/latest-news/florida-rejects-publisers-attempts-to-indoctrinate-students.stml
10 See https://www.nytimes.com/2022/05/07/us/politics/florida-rejected-math-textbooks.html
11 See https://www.wptv.com/news/education/floridas-governor-to-sign-critical-race-theory-education-bill-into-law
12 See https://www.americanbar.org/groups/crsj/publications/human_rights_magazine_home/civil-rights-reimagining-policing/a-lesson-on-critical-race-theory/
13 See https://www.brookings.edu/blog/fixgov/2021/07/02/why-are-states-banning-critical-race-theory/
14 See https://www.pbs.org/newshour/education/so-much-buzz-but-what-is-critical-race-theory
15 See https://www.vanityfair.com/news/2021/07/how-critical-race-theory-mastermind-kimberle-crenshaw-is-weathering-the-culture-wars
16 For race, ethnicity, and geography, see the comprehensive bibliographies curated by Rebecca Futo Kennedy at https://rfkclassics.blogspot.com/p/bibliography-for-race-and-ethnicity-in.html and Aditi Rao at https://classics.barnard.edu/race-and-ethnicity-ancient-mediterranean-world-methods-sources-and-assessments; Padilla Peralta (2015a) and (2015b). For gender and sexuality, see Diotima's compilation of bibliographies at https://diotima-doctafemina.org/bibliographies/; Skinner (2013); Masterson et al. (2018); Ormand (2018); Surtees and Dyer (2020). For ability, see Draycott (2015); Penrose (2015); Laes (2017).
17 See Holmes-Henderson (2021) on access to Classics in English schools being based on 'wealth or luck.' On class see Hall and Stead (2020); Canevaro et al. (2021).
18 Blouin (2017); Konstan (2020).
19 See Agbamu in this volume citing Padilla-Peralta (2019) on issues of inclusivity in publishing scholars from diverse backgrounds, and Leonard in this volume citing Kelly et al. (2019) on gender bias. See also Stewart and Machado (2019) for a case study on inclusivity in publishing focused on the journal *TAPA*.

Works Cited

Adams, E. (2021) 'New Light on "the Viewer": Sensing the Parthenon Galleries in the British Museum', in E. Adams (ed.), *Disability Studies and the Classical Body*, Abingdon, 130–59.

Ahmed, S. (2012) *On Being Included: Racism and Diversity in Institutional Life*, Durham, NC.

Blouin, K. (2017) 'Classical Studies' Glass Ceiling Is White', *Everyday Orientalism*, January 10.
Canevaro, L. et al. (2021) 'If Class Were a Protected Characteristic', *CUCD EDI Blog*, 8th November.
Draycott, J. (2015) 'Reconstructing the Lived Experience of Disability in Antiquity: a Case Study from Roman Egypt', *Greece and Rome* 62.2: 189–205.
Hakkola, L. and Ropers-Huilman, R. (2018) 'A Critical Exploration of Diversity Discourses in Higher Education: A Focus on Diversity in Student Affairs and Admissions', in M. Paulsen (ed.) *Higher Education*, Volume 33, Berlin, 417–68.
Hall, E. and Stead, H. (2020) *A People's History of Classics*, Abingdon.
Holmes-Henderson, A. (2021) 'Access to Classics in English Schools: Confronting Inequalities of Access', *BERA Blog*, 14 July. https://www.bera.ac.uk/blog/classical-subjects-in-english-schools-confronting-inequalities-of-access
Kelly, C. et al. (2019) 'Gender Bias and the Journal of Roman Studies', *Journal of Roman Studies*, 109: 441–8.
Konstan, D. (2020) 'Mapping Diversity in Classical Studies - التنوع معالم في الكلاسيكيات', *Alif: Journal of Comparative Poetics* 40: 9–27.
Kostara, E. (2018) 'Diversity and the Study of the Ancient World', *CUCD Bulletin* 47: 1–10.
Laes, C. (ed.) (2017) *Disability in Antiquity*, Abingdon.
Leonard, V. et al. (2016) 'Women in Classics in the UK: Numbers and Issues', *CUCD Bulletin* 45: 1–17.
Leonard, V. and Lovatt, H. (2020) 'Council of University Classical Departments Equality and Diversity Report 2020', *CUCD EDI Blog*, 1–76.
Masterson, M., Rabinowitz, N. and Robson, J. (eds) (2018) *Sex in Antiquity*, London.
McCoskey, D. (2022) 'Basil Gildersleeve and John Scott: Race and the Rise of American Classical Philology', *American Journal of Philology* 143: 247–77.
Ormand, K. (2018) *Controlling Desires: Sexuality in Ancient Greece and Rome*, Chicago, IL.
Padilla Peralta, D. (2015a) 'Barbarians Inside the Gate, Part I', *Eidolon*, 9 November.
Padilla Peralta, D. (2015b) 'Barbarians Inside the Gate, Part II' *Eidolon*, 12 November.
Padilla Peralta, D. (2019) 'Racial Equity and the Production of Knowledge' [paper presentation], SCS 2019: The Future of Classics, San Diego, CA, 5 January.
Pandey, N. (2021) 'Diversifying Classics in Germany: An Interview With Katharina Wesselmann', *SCS Blog*, 15 April. https://classicalstudies.org/scs-blog/nandini-pandey/blog-diversifying-classics-germany-interview-katharina-wesselmann
Penrose, W. Jr. (2015) 'The Discourse of Disability in Ancient Greece', *Classical World* 108.4: 499–523.

Pineda, P. and Mishra, S. (2022) 'The Semantics of Diversity in Higher Education', *Higher Education*, 1–22.

Rankine, P. (2019) 'The Classics, Race, and Community-Engaged or Public Scholarship', *American Journal of Philology* 140: 345–59.

Rankine, P. (2020) 'Classics for All?: Liberal Education and the Matter of Black Lives', in I. Moyer, A. Lecznar and H. Morse (eds) *Classicisms in the Black Atlantic*, Oxford, 267–90.

Skinner, M. (2013) *Sexuality in Greek and Roman Culture,* Hoboken, NJ.

Stewart, R. and Machado., D. (2019) 'Progress and Precarity: 150 Years of *TAPA*', *TAPA* 149.2: S-39–S-60.

Surtees, A. and Dyer, J. (eds) (2020) *Exploring Gender Diversity in the Ancient World*, Edinburgh.

1 Affectionate Ties

The Discipline of the Classics and the College or University Mission

Patrice Rankine

During the spring semester of 2021, Howard University in Washington, D.C., announced that it was closing its department of Classics, legendary in the American higher education landscape, having formed Toni Morrison and as the department where Frank M. Snowden, Jr., taught for much of the second half of the twentieth century.[1] This news was devastating for many people within the academy and beyond. In Classics circles, petitions circulated to protest the closure, which the administration had threatened for years.[2] On 19 April, the inimitable scholar Cornel West wrote a highly circulated op-ed for *The Washington Post* alongside Jeremy Tate, in which the authors lamented Howard University effectively 'diminishing the light of wisdom and truth that inspired [Frederick] Douglass, [Martin Luther] King[, Jr.], and countless other freedom fighters' (West and Tate 2021). They bemoaned the 'disregard or neglect' of the discipline and of the texts and ideas that it promotes, positioning Classics within 'Western civilization' and the 'Western canon.' They saw the event as a 'spiritual catastrophe.' Contesting this interpretation, on 2 May, Brandon Hogan and Jacoby Adeshei Carter, director of undergraduate studies and chair of philosophy, respectively, responded in *The New York Times*. Whereas Tate and West take a theoretical position, Carter and Hogan argue on the authority of experience. Rather than turning their back on ancient wisdom, these professors assert the continuing importance of Classics within the university's educational offerings. Their 'department [of philosophy] offers seminars on Plato and Aristotle alongside mandatory courses on the history of Africana philosophy' (2021). Rebuffing West, 'who has primarily worked at institutions with huge endowments [relative to Howard's],' they remind their readers that 'departments aren't free.' They view the closure of Classics as a necessary response to a financial dilemma, but they also invoke Howard's broader mission as an underpinning commitment, one deeply rooted in the university's foundation.[3]

As an academic who has served as an administrator at several institutions, happens to be Black, and is also a professor of Classics, I have experienced and absorbed from others the range of discussions and emotions that accompany these kinds of decisions. An academic *discipline*, as the word connotes, demands a kind of devotion, involvement of one's entire self that also speaks to value(s), but there is another site that deserves attention, one to which Carter and Hogan turn, namely the college and university.[4] By considering college and university mission statements, such as that of Howard, and the relationship of units and disciplines to them, in this chapter I probe what the discipline of Classics is or might represent in particular space and time, rather than as an abstraction. Even at institutions where there is not a department of Classics, as is the case at Purdue University, where I taught for 15 years, the cultural discourse around the value of Classics is ubiquitous. Local realities, including college and university cultures and values, dictate that Classics do not ever denote an abstract departmental set of norms. Rather, Classics departments are to a tangible degree specific, the discipline itself inflected in local culture, as we will see in the case studies in this chapter, Howard, Purdue, and Georgetown University. Although I have not taught at Howard or Georgetown, my experiences at Purdue, Hope College, and the University of Richmond frame my understanding of the land grant, Christian, and liberal arts missions. As with Purdue and Georgetown, Howard University foregrounds the evolving meaning of 'the classical' at institutions of higher education in the US and the relationship of this meaning to other cultural sites of significance, including race and Blackness, the humanities, and Western or non-Western discourse.[5] As was the case with Tate and West's take on Howard, the classical has often been taken to signify a kind of universalism, and for this reason, its demise can result in lament. Rather than a cipher for universalism, something more particular, akin to what Emily Greenwood (2013) calls 'omni-local' is evident in these examples. Omni-localism, as the term suggests, places any claims to universalism within a specific setting. Any purported universalism of Classics confronts the local concerns of given persons, groups, or institutions.

The life of an academic department, or disciplinary affiliation, is affective, amounting to a substantial portion of the identity of individuals who inhabit it. The mission, as an articulation of the broader college or university culture, can also have a strong affective pull—and it should.[6] Mission statements can be read quite generically, as if the same consultants were hired to craft the language.[7] At Howard, the mission statement's racial inflection focuses on the university' scope of action. Tate and West cited Black 'freedom fighters' in their defense of the Classics.[8] Carter and Hogan also invoked the broader interests of Black people, specifically students. In the end, each party's arguments would have to focus on Classics' efficacy for Black people, given the broader mission of the institution with which they were concerned. Tate and West, however, present another interest, namely 'Western civilization,' whose light the closure of Classics, was diminishing. Theirs is also an affective argument, as the idea of 'spiritual decay' or 'moral decline' corroborates. Carter and Hogan, asking the question of how best to accomplish Howard's mission, invest their emotions elsewhere, although they affirm the continued importance of classical texts to the education of Black people. The opposing arguments were only the most recent iteration of a longstanding debate among Black educators about the best role for Classics in the mission of Historically Black Colleges and Universities (HBCUs).[9]

Howard University: Historically Black College and University

Founded in 1867, Howard's stated mission in 2020 was that of a 'historically Black private university' that 'provides an educational experience of exceptional quality at the undergraduate, graduate, and professional levels to students of high academic standing and potential, with particular emphasis upon educational opportunities for Black students.'[10] Many HBCUs in the US developed out of the Morrill Acts of 1862 and 1890: Georgia State Industrial Institute for Colored Youth, for example, out of the first (Goings and O'Connor 2015), and Tuskegee and North Carolina A&T buttressed by the second.[11] I will discuss the Morrill Act below in relation to Purdue. In the case of Howard, congressional grants endowed a seminary for the training of Black clergy. The institution gained private funding and was named after Oliver Otis Howard, an American Civil War veteran and one-time commissioner of the Freedman's Bureau. Although some HBCUs were in existence before 1862, scores began to open in the years following the Civil War. Black colleges and universities were to respond to the nineteenth-century calls for Emancipation and the Industrial Revolution. After the Civil War, some four million formerly enslaved Black people entered the American economy as talent, creators, and potential wage earners.[12]

Within this landscape, the department of Classics would have struck a minor—albeit important, historically—chord. The major chord had been the uplift of Black people in the US and to some extent globally, within the framework of classical Western humanism. As Kenneth Goings and Eugene O'Connor argue, Black leaders in the nineteenth and early twentieth centuries believed that the Classics were their own, citing Egypt and ancient African accomplishments as their lineage (2015). As a concept, 'the West' might be even more fraught in the twenty-first century than it was at its apogee in the late nineteenth century (Appiah 2006). There is a burgeoning discourse among Black writers, ranging from Frank B. Wilderson (2020) to Zakiyyah Iman Jackson (2020), that questions whether people who have been 'Black[ened]' can ever be successfully reconciled to the West. These writers bracket the '[ened]' to emphasize race as a fiction, fabrication, and social process, not determined once-and-for-all but plastic, or moveable. Their idea is that Black people had always been a construction of the West, questioning whether such a being could ever be reconciled to it. Whereas classical humanism assumes an expansiveness and a broadening of people admitted into it (During 2021), these writers question humanism itself owing to an unredeemable genealogy. This is not the place for arguments for or against classical humanism, but given the relationship between Black(ened) people and the West that slavery exacerbated, it is no wonder that it would be an object of scrutiny. In the 1960s at Howard, Snowden, the classical humanist, would meet opposition from the students demonstrating in the wake of the murder of Martin Luther King, Jr (Bernstein 2007; Fox 2007). The issue was not so much that Snowden was a classicist. Rather, the deeper concern was the link between his classicism and his integrationist stance, his trust in the fairness of the broader American population once they saw that Black people were educable. The arguments for assimilation did not convince the young protestors. They were fed up with the second-class status that, even after integration and the granting of civil rights, rendered the funding of foreign wars more strategically significant than the uplift of domestic urban populations. Snowden's demise as Dean at Howard would be only the most relevant in a longstanding, internal debate among African Americans about the efficacy of assimilation over various forms of militancy. As such, debates over the best forms of education might sometimes obscure the broader goal of Black uplift. Even at the end of the nineteenth century, into the early twentieth century, Booker T. Washington and W. E. B. Du Bois debated the best path for the education of formerly enslaved people, Du Bois arguing for classical humanism as essential to the edification of people formerly deemed property. Washington's position that technical training was the best lifeline for the formerly enslaved Black masses had as its end the best interest of the same, not the abstract question about the best form of education, everywhere and always (Gasman and McMickens 2010).[13]

From 1867 to the twenty-first century, despite limited resources, Howard served a broad constituency: undergraduate, graduate, and professional levels. Hogan and Carter demonstrate an awareness of the strategic, mission-oriented questions that went into the decision to close the university's department of Classics. As they put it, 'Howard students are reading Parmenides, John Locke and Jean-Jacques Rousseau along with Angela Davis, Charles Mills, and Franz Fanon. Students will continue to read Shakespeare and Walt Whitman alongside Toni Morrison and James Baldwin.' Rather than spiritual decline, closing the Classics department signaled a 'Renaissance' that includes 'majors in interdisciplinary humanities (which incorporates classical studies courses), bioethics, international affairs, and environmental studies.' In this case, the classical is called to bear witness to non-humanistic, contemporary concerns. Carter and Hogan situated Howard, as an HBCU, within the longue durée of American higher education, where these institutions were late in building wealth, compared to institutions like Harvard, and limited in scope.[14] Howard's limited resources render all educational decisions something of a zero-sum proposition, focused on practical outcomes rather than ideal scenarios.

Within its limited resources, Howard's mission historically responds to a particular gap and need in the American higher education landscape. A question that Hogan and Carter raise is that of how the ideas, texts, and concerns that formed Classics can continue to shape and be shaped within Howard's environment. They cite bioethics as an excellent example of an area of interest that might best serve Black students in the twenty-first century. As philosophers, Carter and Hogan would be the first to note the centrality of Greek thinkers to questions of the human in relation to technology and the environment, but they might also include in the conversation texts and thinkers outside of the Western canon who might not immediately come to mind for many audiences trained in Classics. Howard University stands apart among colleges and universities that offer Greco-Roman Classics in *requiring* students to study Africana philosophy alongside these Western offerings. This requirement serves as the beginning of a corrective to the Black[ened] personhood that the Western civilization created.

An objection that has been raised to anything less than departmental status for Classics at Howard is that with meager course offerings, Howard cannot train students with an interest in pursuing the discipline as future professionals in the field. In a *New York Times* article of April 25, 2021, students cite this issue. The department's dissolution, according to one student, 'would prevent the in-depth study of Classics and could inhibit Black students from pursuing the field as scholars.' The student's concern raises the question of whether enrollees were clamoring for a minor or concentration in the Greco-Roman Classics in the first place.[15] Dissolving the department certainly forecloses the option of in-depth study for students, but an administrative counterargument is understandably that the students were not flocking to the discipline in the first place. There was not 'a huge pipeline of Black students that are being prevented from entering the academic field for Classics.' And departments cost money. Howard faces the same struggles as other institutions with low-enrolled, less-sought-after subjects. In many cases, course sharing across institutions, which technology affords, is an imperfect but practical approach.

The closing of the department might not be the spiritual crisis that Tate and West declare, but in a perfect world, Howard might well have missed an opportunity to become a site where such a pipeline of Black students into the Classics could exist, if this is a desirable end, and their arguments to support this, including those of Du Bois and West. The students point to an important contribution that such a pipeline would have created: representation. I had the privilege of delivering the Frank M. Snowden lecture for the department of Classics at Howard in 2010. More memorable than the lecture itself was the conversation with students that ensued afterward. The curiosity and hunger for knowledge were palpable. As can be imagined, students were as interested in why I, a Black man, would choose the profession of teaching and researching in Classics, and they were as interested in connections across the ancient Mediterranean as they were in Parmenides or Plato. Representation is itself a pathway, occasioning new questions and focal points, different concerns, and approaches. Even without a department of Classics, Howard supports a rigorous study of the past, one that could still lead to entry into the professional field of classical studies if a student should so choose. The mission of Howard University, however, calls into question whether a department of Classics can truly thrive under the institution's current financial constraints and where the mission includes even a fraction of the commitment to the education of Black students that is central to HBCUs. The end to which intellectuals from Du Bois to Washington, West to Carter strive, namely the prosperity of Black(ened) people, has not been broadly shown to be attained by a department of Classics, although studying the Classics remains part of its missional identity.

Small Teaching: Classics at Purdue University

Like many humanistic disciplines, Classics can play a role in the broader purposes of higher education, but the discipline has no pride of place, independent of the claim to have been a site of origins.[16] Classics, for example, can play a role in 'small teaching' (Lang 2021). Liberal arts colleges often boast a small student-to-faculty ratio, which increases the chances that young people striving to find themselves and their passions will have a supportive environment in which to achieve their goals. There is ample evidence that this support has several positive outcomes, including immediate retention and long-term success in the students' chosen professional fields and beyond.[17] Departments of Classics across the country support this broader institutional mission of all institutions of higher education, whether research institutions or liberal arts colleges. Classics, where small student-to-faculty ratios are the norm, is representative of small teaching, as defined by James L. Lang, although he includes a myriad of classroom techniques for learning available to many disciplines.

Liberal arts colleges might come to mind as being best able to achieve the student-to-faculty ratio best for small teaching, but Classics and other humanities can thrive in many other environments. Purdue is a place seemingly as far from the liberal arts mission as one might imagine. Founded in 1869, Purdue was born out of the Congressional Morrill Land Grant of 1862. The Land Grant Act was aimed at the 'endowment, support, and maintenance of at least one college where the leading object shall be, without excluding other scientific and classical studies, and including military tactics, to teach such branches of learning as are related to agriculture and the mechanic arts, in such manner as the legislatures of the States may respectively prescribe, in order to promote the liberal and practical education of the industrial classes in the several pursuits and professions of life.'[18] The language of the Act specified that this learning was to occur 'without excluding other scientific and classical studies,' but a foundational distinction was drawn between technical training (which by the early twenty-first century would become Science, Technology, Engineering, and Mathematics, or STEM) and humanistic education.[19] The Morrill Act was part of a postwar effort to galvanize American industries in the wake of the free, uneducated labor that slavery afforded.

When I arrived in 1998, there was no department of Classics, and there still is not. Rather, the College of Liberal Arts had an interdisciplinary program in Classics, which drew from various departments, including History, Philosophy, and Foreign Languages and Literatures

(FLL), later renamed the School of Languages and Culture (SLC). Within SLC, there is a department of Arabic, Classics, Hebrew, and Italian (ACHI). Classics, in fact, *decreased* its full-time equivalency (FTE) as it gained status within a formal department, as a result of the battle of esteem that often occurs between units and their administrators. Nevertheless, individual classicists continue to do important work at Purdue. If disciplinarity is affective, we might think of the work humanists do at Purdue as fugitivity, which links this work to a kind of radicalism. That is, more subversive work can be done using indirect tactics than frontal assaults. In my case, I was able to publish a range of work that came to challenge students and academics in Classics and beyond because I was not limited by the constraints of someone trained and hired to teach in a specific niche within the discipline. My first book, *Ulysses in Black: Ralph Ellison, Classicism, and African American Literature,* was a product of this environment. With this as my primary monograph, I undoubtedly would have been denied tenure at most Classics departments in the country at the time. (I might have fared well in the UK, among colleagues pioneering the field of classical reception studies, with whom I began working closely after the book's publication.[20]) Purdue's example speaks to the transformative potential of Classicists and other scholars who remain at Howard University in the wake of its closure.

In the case of Purdue, a university of 43,000 students, faculties are separated into Colleges, e.g., the College of Liberal Arts, each with a degree of autonomy over its own graduation requirements. Classics is an extremely small player within this landscape, with single-digit majors in any given year. Most of the enrollment in these classes consists of students who need credits to fulfill a requirement in their major. Much to the lament of many faculty members in CLA, these credits are often not language requirements because many colleges have done away with these.[21] Notwithstanding the university's technological and agricultural focus, in my experience at Purdue, the crisis of humanistic education of which Classics is a part is no more acutely felt than at those institutions designated as liberal arts colleges. For example, at Hope College, where I served as Dean for the Humanities and Arts from 2013 to 2016, the most subscribed majors were engineering, business, and nursing, evidence that even at liberal arts colleges students are feeling the pressure to be practical. Their tuition and time spent not drawing a salary must pay off. The drop in enrollment in humanistic classes should be read within the same broader cultural landscape. In fall 2008, 6,657 students were enrolled in the College of Liberal Arts at Purdue; in fall 2019, that number dropped to 2,595.[22] While humanistic education suffers these losses, the number for Engineering rose from 6,579 to 9,413 during the same ten-year span. Engineering now only requires two communication courses during the first year. The 4,000+ students enrolled in the College of Science, however, 'are expected to develop an understanding of at least one other culture in addition to their own through learning a language, taking culture and/ or diversity courses, or participating in an approved Study Abroad experience.'[23] In addition to the three-semester language requirement, courses in Classical Studies and Latin are listed among those that satisfy the culture and/or diversity requirement.

Small teaching puts educators like Classicists in the best position to support the success of students, whatever the missional inflection of the institutions they serve. When I arrived at Purdue, given its agricultural and technological focus, I imagined myself developing a curriculum in 'practical' Liberal Arts, where I might teach courses about agriculture as an ancient practice, views of technology among Greek and Roman authors, or even ethics courses that might be of benefit to Business students. In keeping with the idea of small teaching, these were not the courses students necessarily wanted or needed. Many already had an ideal notion of college education, drawn from such popular representations as Robin Williams' character in *Dead Poets' Society* (1989), the inspiring teacher who pours his (also problematic) passions into students, standing on desks to emphasize his point. Such performative professors did draw students into the classroom. Classical mythology and ancient history classes attracted over 200 students each semester. At the same time, where the Classicist had their deeper impact was in the mentoring and close relationship with students across the spectrum, both those studying in the field and the broader array of engineers and others with whom we formed lasting relationships. The Purdue Gallup Poll points to one significant relationship between a student and faculty member, whether a research project or mentoring relationship, as critical to lifelong success.[24] Students could find this relationship among the Classicists.

Students studying with Classicists face a similar challenge at Purdue as those at Howard. As at many institutions, a degree of ingenuity is necessary to support students who need to supplement the education they receive. If, for example, students care to pursue advanced degrees in the field, scaffolding is necessary. Scholars seeking departmental homes might also prefer a place with a full department of Classics and the ability to offer a range of subjects. Whatever the case, the openness and freedom of the environment at Purdue allowed me to pioneer subfields, like Black Classicism and Classical Reception Studies, and to expand the reach of the discipline. Allied programs such as Comparative Literature and Philosophy brought advanced undergraduates and serious graduate students who sought out instruction in Greek and Latin. Classics could claim a life at Purdue that was vibrant, if not central or critical to the university's mission in obvious ways. Being in Classics at an institution like Purdue can be an act of fugitivity, where faculty are able to find purpose and meaning, even without departmental status. The fugitive (the professor) hides and does their work within the broader territory of the university and its mission not so much undermining the mission, but finding space within it.

Cura Personalis: Georgetown University and Missional Decision-Making

The third and final case study of college and university missions and their potential relationship to the disciplines and texts within Classical Studies is directly *missional*. By one definition, missional colleges and universities are those recognized to have at their core a commitment to a purported original Christian commitment of all higher education in the US. Several institutions and their affiliates, such as the Lilly Endowment and the Council for Christian Colleges and Universities, might be considered in this vein, and their rootedness in Christianity underscores a broader relationship to Western culture upon which these institutions call. There are certainly problematic aspects to these claims, as we saw in the example of Cornel West's claim of 'spiritual catastrophe.' Within the context of claims to tradition, the Classics take on a heightened significance. West spent a good portion of his career teaching at Union Theological Seminary in New York City, and his exegesis of 'the West' seamlessly weaves together Greco-Roman texts and references with Judeo-Christian ones. His reading of Howard University's closure of the department of Classics as a 'spiritual catastrophe' that threatens to snuff out the 'wisdom and truth' of the West is best read in this light. The religious bent of the claim is as much affective as it is historical. One becomes wise by studying wisdom traditions, but West discusses Western traditions exclusively.

In a broader sense, missional institutions maintain a semblance of their original charter—even 'land grant' comes to take on a different inflection when the institution is no longer the only public option within the region—while still crafting new goals and actions built upon the past. Tradition is elastic and can bend to its new environment. Georgetown University, 'a Catholic and Jesuit, student-centered research university' in Washington, D.C., is just such an example. The relationship between 'Catholic and Jesuit' and 'the new republic,' alongside the 'commitment to justice and the common good,' plays out in particular ways.[25]

A central Jesuit principle is the *cura personalis*, which derives from the Platonic notion of the care of the self, or *epimeleia heautou*. Georgetown's missional idea of the care of the self is rooted in the past, but it met a challenging crossroads in the early twenty-first century. On 1 September 2016, John J. DeGioia, President of Georgetown University in Washington, D.C., announced that the university community would take steps to redress the legacy of the trafficking of human slaves, in which it historically participated. Serious and somber, President DeGioia used sacral language that not only resonated with Georgetown's Jesuit mission, but his words had a meaningful reach beyond their Christian rooting. He referred to the school's Jesuit stewards' participation in 1838 in the trafficking of Black(ened) people, who had arrived in this country in shackles from Africa, as an 'original sin.' The sin yielded strange, though profitable, fruit. From the horror of the massive sale of 272 African souls on 19 June 1838, Georgetown gained, in the currency of DeGioia's day, $3.3 million. Founded in 1789, Georgetown held a $1.5 billion endowment in 2016. When Georgetown's news broke, outlets broadcasted DeGioia's comments, during which the leader promised to 'draw upon resources of the Catholic tradition' to make amends for the school's past. In a vision rooted in the school's original mission, President DeGioia offered a 'mass of reconciliation.' Among the immediate actions Georgetown would take were: renaming two buildings, one for an African American slave, a second for a black educator; building a public memorial, which would acknowledge the school's role in slavery; and establishing an admission policy for the descendants of the slaves sold in 1838, which at first blush resembles legacy admissions impacting generations of alumni. Georgetown University, President DeGioia asserted, could no longer 'hide from the truth.'

Whatever it was before 1 September 2016, President DeGioia on that day proved Georgetown University to be a purposeful missional community. No doubt, the community included the members of the task force that delivered the report, which issued the call for meaningful dialogue on slavery, a treatment of the history of particular sites on campus, and recommendations on 'how best to acknowledge and recognize the University's historical relationship to the institution of slavery.'[26] Without painting a utopian picture of concordance, the Georgetown community that must carry out this vision includes their faculty, staff, alumni, and every student who attends the university.[27]

Whatever the individual responses, however, no one within or outside of the institution could reasonably argue against the evident attempt to align Georgetown University's mission, born out of its past, with its vision for the future.

Judging from its website, Georgetown houses a ten-member department of Classics with majors and minors at the undergraduate level. Although there are no graduate studies, a post-baccalaureate program provides students with 'the opportunity to improve their knowledge of Ancient Greek and Latin.' On its website, the department cites the connection between the Jesuit mission and its own: 'The study of the cultures of ancient Greece and Rome through their languages has been at the core of humanistic learning for centuries, and constitutes the heart of both the Jesuit tradition and the liberal arts curriculum.'[28] The department has a tremendous opportunity to rely on the university's mission for its direction.

Death and Life: Some Concluding Thoughts

In each of the cases above, professors and administrators at colleges and universities in the US can be seen to grapple with the life of a specific discipline, in this case that of Classics, within the broader institutional mission. As Hogan and Carter (2021) put it regarding Classics at Howard University, departments cost money. Financial considerations can make the life of a discipline feel like a zero-sum proposition, but if all parties invested in the conversation consider the college or university mission, meaningful work is inevitable. This position presupposes a serious mission that has an affective pull, not boilerplate, corporate language. It is worth noting, moreover, that this emotional pull might also be *dis*affection. Just as many HBCUs continued to instruct in the Classics despite the opposition of many of their white trustees, the discipline can thrive in places where departments have been destroyed and intellectual engagement is under assault. As the examples show (Goings and O'Connor 2010 and 2015), Classics can continue to surreptitiously serve the curriculum, even with the death of a self-standing department. Time will tell if this is the case at Howard University. Limited resources determine whether the university would hire a professional Classicist outside of the departmental structure. That said, gaining status within a broader self-standing department at Purdue University did not correlate to increased FTE but rather coincided with a reduction in personnel dedicated to the discipline. On the other side, if Classics continues to retool itself for the times, including training professionals to know and understand the ancient world beyond Greece and Rome, including not only Egypt but areas like Kush and Subsaharan Africa, it can prove more adaptable at institutions like Howard University. The university's commitment to Africana interests could include the study of an ancient world framed beyond Greece and Rome.

As institutions with long legacies in the West, all colleges and universities have the potential to have the kind of missional pull of Georgetown University. The relationship between this affective tie and one's discipline is of as much importance as the extra-institutional shape the discipline takes, e.g., how it moves within structures like the Society for Classical Studies, in the case of Classics. As I have offered, my argument presupposes that disciplines involve our affections; they must, given that discipline is corporeal. I am not advocating that academicians displace any loyalty we may feel from the discipline to the institution, but such loyalty is consistently under duress, especially when it pertains to underrepresented scholars with already troubled relationships with our chosen fields. It is understandable that disaffection and disaffiliation have been increasingly advocated, even to the extent that new, critical approaches to existing disciplines are being proposed (Umachandran 2022). Blind loyalty, whether to the discipline or the institution, is inadvisable. At the same time, recognizing the affective pull of disciplinary affiliation allows the academic to make conscious choices, including ways of calling disciplines into conversation with the college or university mission. Indiscipline, or fugitivity, can be productive as long as scholars recognize that lack of affection might point to more deep-seeded questions.

Notes

1 On Morrison, see Rankine (2006) and Roynon (2014); for Snowden, see Parmenter (2021). For Snowden obituaries, see Bernstein (2007) and Fox (2007).
2 The ongoing crisis in funding and priority of arts and humanities fields like Classics is well-known, but as it pertains to Historically Black Colleges and Universities from the nineteenth into mid-twentieth centuries, see Goings and O'Connor (2010 and 2015).
3 For these foundations, see Goings and O'Connor (2010 and 2015).
4 I realize that disciplinarity itself—what areas of study constitute the discipline—should be in question and am sympathetic toward the critique of the discipline of Classics in Umachandran (2022). A commitment to *indiscipline*, critique, or notions of failure, as argued in Halberstam (2011), is not only useful, but healthy. While I also find Harney and Moten (2013) compelling, I worry about the underlying cynicism of the survival techniques implied in the position of fugitivity. More on this last proposition throughout this chapter.
5 On the relative newness of the discourse of the West, see Appiah (2016).

6 Within my broader argument is a call for strong, differentiated college and university mission statements, assertions that should be easy to locate on the college or university websites. Differentiation is an ongoing challenge among colleges and universities, who are for the most part chasing the same 'market' of students. See Selingo (2020) as an example of the recurring conversation about mission and differentiation.
7 On distinctions among mission statements as public or private, normative or aspirational, see Morphew and Hartley (2006).
8 For a similar perspective, see Goings and O'Connor (2010 and 2015). They cite David Walker's 'Appeal to the Colored Citizens of the World' (1829) as reliant upon Greek and Roman tropes in its radicalism, Walker himself the quintessential freedom fighter.
9 Interestingly, this debate was not always straightforward or well-intended. Goings and O'Connor (2015) argue that white people during the Reconstruction period denied Black people access to the Classics because they deemed these former slaves unworthy of such refinements. Black educators, in their view, had consistently supported some form of classical education for their students.
10 Go to https://www2.howard.edu/about/mission, last accessed 20/07/22.
11 On mission statements of HBCUs, see Gasman and McMickens (2010). I am thankful to Tryan L. McMickens for points of clarification and for reading an early draft of this chapter.
12 Go to https://www.statista.com/statistics/1010169/black-and-slave-population-us-1790-1880/, last accessed 20/07/22.
13 Goings and O'Connor (2015) argue that this was the same interest of Black leaders on both sides of the education debate, whether Du Bois' position or that of Washington.
14 Other universities founded in the nineteenth century (such as the University of Richmond) are relatively wealthy, so the argument of longevity does not work on its own. As McMickens pointed out in our conversation, it is also ill-advised to compare ivy league institutions to any others, including HBCUs to ivies.
15 The article titled Howard's Classics department as a 'hub for Black scholarship.' I see no evidence for such a claim.
16 This is not to dismiss claims of origin wholesale, which had a cultural cache and continues to. See Goings and O'Connor (2015) for the centrality of Black American claims to classical origins to their advocacy for classical education. From another perspective, Soyinka (1990) is an example of the critique of European claims of origins, which pertain to literacy and the written record of traditions. Soyinka takes on the claim to the Athenian origins of drama.
17 Since (2014), for example, Purdue has released a Gallup Index on learning outcomes. Go to https://www.purdue.edu/newsroom/gallup/reports.html, last accessed 20/07/22.
18 Go to https://www.archives.gov/milestone-documents/morrill-act, last accessed 20/07/22.
19 Louis Menand (2021) reveals the real dynamics behind the artificial conflict. Flattening any distinction between the sciences and the humanities, Menand argues that 'knowledge is a tool, not a state of being.' He quips that 'the idea that students develop a greater capacity for empathy by

reading books in literature classes about people who never existed than they can by taking classes in fields that study actual human behavior does not make a lot of sense.'

20 I am forever indebted to Edith Hall for my first invitation to a conference at Royal Holloway commemorating the 200th anniversary of the Slave Trade Act of 1807.
21 For example, the College of Engineering does not require a language major, whereas the College of Liberal Arts does.
22 For these and other statistics, go to https://www.purdue.edu/enrollment management/data-reports/index.php, last accessed 20/07/22.
23 See https://www.purdue.edu/science/Current_Students/curriculum_and_degree_requirements/language-and-culture.html, last accessed 20/07/22.
24 One former student who majored in Pharmaceutical Studies recently wrote: 'I still remember how awesome your class was at Purdue!' Another major in Classical Studies who went on to earn an MBA, and is working in accounts receivable, is 'doing great. I love my new job, and the people I work with are A LOT like me which is something I have never run into.'
25 For the full mission statement, see https://governance.georgetown.edu/mission-statement/, last accessed 20/07/22.
26 The report is readily available online at slavery.georgetown.edu. Georgetown is part of a group of Universities Studying Slavery, founded at the University of Virginia and also public at slavery.virginia.edu.
27 There were a range of responses within their community, dependent upon the experiences, perspectives, and political orientation of its members. See Swarns (2021).
28 Go to https://classics.georgetown.edu/history/, last accessed 20/07/22.

Works Cited

Appiah, K.A. (2016) 'There Is No Such Thing as Western Civilisation', *The Guardian*, 9 November.

Bernstein, A. (2007) 'Frank Snowden', *The Washington Post*, 22 February.

During, S. (2021) '"Whiteness" and the Humanities: An Impasse', *The Chronicle of Higher Education*, 2 September.

Fox, M. (2007) 'Frank M. Snowden Jr., 95, Historian of Blacks in Antiquity, Dies', *The New York Times*, 28 February.

Gasman, M. and McMickens, T.L. (2010) 'Liberal or Professional Education? The Mission of Public Black Colleges and Universities and Their Impact on the Future of African Americans', *Souls* 12: 286–305.

Goings, K. and O'Connor, E. (2010) 'Lessons Learned: The Role of the Classics at Black Colleges and Universities', *The Journal of Negro Education* 79.4: 521–31.

Goings, K. and O'Connor, E. (2015) 'The Classical Curriculum at Black Colleges and Universities and the Roles of Various Missionary Aid Societies', *BICS Supplement* 128: 75–96.

Greenwood, E. (2013) 'Afterword: Omni-Local Classical Receptions', *Classical Receptions Journal* 5: 354–61.

Halberstam, J. (2011) *The Queer Art of Failure*, Durham.

Harney, S. and Moten, F. (2013) *The Undercommons: Fugitive Planning & Black Study*, New York, NY.

Hogan, B. and Carter, J.A. (2021) 'There's No Classics "Catastrophe" at Howard University', *The New York Times*, 2 May.

Jackson, Z.I. (2020) *Becoming Human: Matter and Meaning in an Antiblack World*, New York, NY.

Koch, F. and Bratvold, R. (2011) 'Game Theory in the Oil and Gas Industry', *The Way Ahead*, 14 January.

Lang, J.M. (2021) *Small Teaching: Everyday Lessons from the Science of Learning*, 2nd ed., Hoboken, NJ.

Menand, L. (2021) 'What's So Great About Great-Books Courses', *The New Yorker*, 20 December.

Morphew, C.C. and Hartley, M. (2006) 'Mission Statements: A Thematic Analysis of Rhetoric Across Institutional Type', *The Journal of Higher Education* 77: 456–71.

Parmenter, C.S. (2021) '"A Happy Coincidence": Race, the Cold War, and Frank M. Snowden, Jr's Blacks in Antiquity', *Classical Receptions Journal*, 13: 485–506.

Rankine, P.D. (2006) *Ulysses in Black: Ralph Ellison, Classicism, and African American Literature*, Madison, WI.

Roynon, T. (2014) *Toni Morrison and the Classical Tradition: Transforming American Culture*, Oxford.

Selingo, J.J. (2020) 'Colleges Need to Rethink Their Market – and Maybe Their Mission', *The Chronicle of Higher Education*, 16 February.

Soyinka, W. (1990) *Myth, Literature and the African World*, Cambridge.

Swarns, R.L. (2016) 'Georgetown University Plans Steps to Atone for Slave Past', *The New York Times*, 1 September.

Swarns, R.L. (2021) 'Catholic Order Pledges $100 Million to Atone for Slave Labor and Sales', *The New York Times*, 15 March.

Umachandran, M. (2022) 'Disciplinecraft: Towards an Anti-Racist Classics', *TAPhA* 152: 25–31.

Waller, A. (2021) 'Howard Students Protest Cut of Classics Department, Hub for Black Scholarship', *The New York Times*, 25 April.

West, C. and Tate, J. (2021) 'Howard University's Removal of Classics Is a Spiritual Catastrophe', *The Washington Post*, 19 April.

Wilderson, F.B.I.I.I. (2020) *Afropessimism*, New York, NY.

2 Digging Deeper
Toward a More Inclusive Archaeology of the Ancient Mediterranean

Nadhira Hill

Introduction

Questions of whether, when, where, and how to better recruit, support, and mentor scholars of color have been considered on both sides of the Atlantic for several years now, with individuals, departments, and professional institutions in anthropology, philology, ancient history, and the archaeology of the ancient Mediterranean engaging in diversity, equity, inclusion, and accessibility (DEIA) work to varying degrees. In general, the efforts of these groups ramped up considerably in the wake of the murders of George Floyd, Breonna Taylor, Ahmaud Arbery, and many other Black men, women, and children, resulting in sustained Black Lives Matter protests beginning in summer 2020. The systemic injustices and barriers to access and retention deeply embedded in these fields of study, however, are not new.

Despite this, comprehensive demographic data remains virtually non-existent for archaeologists working in the ancient Mediterranean. Many diversity and inclusion initiatives have been developed by individuals and organizations over the last five years. This implies that a not insignificant number of archaeologists in this field come from historically excluded groups. A panel featuring archaeologists of color, held on 3 March 2022, aimed to build on previous diversity and inclusion work by foregrounding the experiences of archaeologists of color working in the Mediterranean and by providing guidance on how both individuals and institutions can continue supporting both prospective and current archaeologists of color.

Outlining the Problem

Several people have pointed out that Classics and related fields are overwhelmingly white (Blouin 2017; White and Draycott 2020; Poser 2021). In 1992, Melinda A. Zeder and colleagues were asked by the

Executive Board of the Society for American Archaeology (SAA) to design a Census that would 'build a detailed and comprehensive picture not just of the SAA membership, but of [the] profession as well' (Zeder 1997, 1). Only 2 out of 1,600 respondents self-identified as Black (Zeder 1997; Agbe-Davies 2014; Flewellyn et al. 2021), 4 as being of Asian heritage, 15 as Hispanic, and 10 as Native American. The results of the SAA survey in addition to personal communication prompted Maria Franklin to consider some possible reasons for the low numbers of Black archaeologists in the field. On the one hand, Black Americans tend to be more attracted to careers 'where they may have more immediate effects' on their own communities, such as in the fields of business, medicine, and law (Franklin 1997, 800). On the other, public perception of archaeology – including who does archaeology and where – tends to obscure archaeology's potential as a powerful tool for uncovering black histories and empowering black communities.

An equivalent survey has not been conducted for the Archaeological Institute of America (AIA). By contrast, when the Society for Classical Studies (SCS) compared the data from surveys conducted in 2004 and 2014, they argued that the sample size was too small to draw statistically meaningful conclusions about the representation of minorities in the profession. This statement alone, however, illustrates the problematic homogeneity of the field. The situation is different for the data on the representation of historically excluded groups among students. There was greater representation at the undergraduate and graduate levels than at the faculty level. Despite this, students from underrepresented groups tend to be less likely to continue on to PhD programs than students who identify as white.

According to a 2018 survey conducted by the SCS on harassment and discrimination, of 728 incidents, 14.7% of them involved discrimination or harassment related to one's ethnicity, and 7.4% related to one's race (SCS 2018). A total of 44.4% of these incidents occurred while the respondent was a graduate student, while nearly half (49.2%) happened somewhere in their faculty path (i.e., while a junior, contingent, or senior faculty member). For undergraduate (58.1%) and graduate students (62.8%), a majority of these incidents were perpetrated by a professor. This is not an insignificant phenomenon, especially when one considers the power differentials at play. In light of this, it is likely that student victims tend to be less inclined to report incidents of discrimination or harassment. Among the reasons for not recommending that others report similar incidents, 68.7% of 2018 SCS survey respondents cited possible 'negative professional repercussions';

60.6% cited the possibility of 'retaliation'; and 51.5% selected the option relating to 'stress, anxiety, or mental distress.'

Equivalent data is difficult to find for archaeology, especially archaeology of the ancient Mediterranean. As with the SCS surveys, a common difficulty is the low number of respondents to surveys from under-represented groups (Clancy et al. 2014; Viglione 2020). Despite the lack of data on identity-based harassment in the field, the work done by individuals at several institutions to develop guidelines for inclusive fieldwork environments suggests that it is not uncommon (e.g., Demery and Pipkin 2020).

Finding Solutions

Increased attention has been given to these issues in the years following the Black Lives Matter protests in 2020. In particular, there have been more studies and discussions surrounding more covert, structural issues relating to racism and exclusion in anthropology, philology, ancient history, and the archaeology of the ancient Mediterranean. The most sustained efforts have come from professional organizations either closely related to anthropology or based in Europe.

Following a 2020 webinar titled 'Archaeology in the Time of Black Lives Matter,'[1] the Society of Black Archaeologists (SBA) launched a program of virtual events that aimed to combat the pervasive anti-Black and anti-Indigenous attitudes in archaeology by promoting the voices and work of archaeologists who identify as Black, Indigenous, or persons of color (BIPOC). Much of this work has been collaborative. In particular, the 2020–2021 SAPIENS webinar series on 'Black and Indigenous Futures in Archaeology' was co-organized by the SBA, the Indigenous Archaeology Collective, the Cornell Institute of Archaeology and Material Studies (CIAMS), the Wenner-Gren Foundation for Anthropological Research, and SAPIENS.

Most recently, in 2022, the SBA collaborated with the Cornell Institute of Archaeology and Material Sciences (CIAMS) and the Indigenous Archaeology Collective on a companion podcast to SAPIENS season 4 (Our Past is Our Future). The companion podcast is called 'Sapiens Talk Back: Changing Archaeology's Stories and Who Tells Them.' In 'Sapiens Talk Back,' students and scholars from various institutions have extended discussions that build on SAPIENS season 4 and explore new perspectives on how Black and Indigenous voices are changing how archaeology tells its stories and who tells them.

Some organizations have also offered blueprints for more inclusive practices in the field of archaeology. The manifesto written by members of the European Society of Black and Allied Archaeologists (ESBAA) in 2021 contributes to this conversation by doing two things. The first part of the manifesto identifies 'fundamental barriers that have a profound impact on the ability to access the profession and enjoy a fruitful career progression' (Brunache et al. 2021, 294–5). These barriers are organized into three categories or areas of impact: access and recruitment; retention and support; and mentoring and allyship. The second part includes a call to action and provides preliminary practices that archaeologists can begin to implement in order to effect structural and systemic change in the field.

Equivalent work in institutions for scholars in Classical Studies and Classical archaeology has been more intermittent. To date nothing equivalent to the ESBAA manifesto has been published; most of this work has taken the form of webinars, roundtables, panels, and paper sessions at conferences. In August 2020, the AIA sponsored a three-part series of webinars titled 'Critical Conversations on Race, Teaching, and Antiquity.' The webinars aimed to provide concrete strategies, approaches, and resources that educators could use to promote inclusivity in courses on the ancient Mediterranean. Panels and paper sessions centered on topics relating to diversity and inclusion in the ancient and modern worlds have been increasingly prevalent at the annual joint meetings of the AIA and SCS. At the 2022 meeting, there were sessions concerning inclusive approaches to vase painting; activisms in the ancient and modern worlds; and inclusive assessment in the classroom.

Although the SCS itself has not sponsored any events or webinars related to DEIA, an affiliated organization, the Women's Classical Caucus (WCC), has filled this void by hosting numerous events since 2021. Many early WCC events centered on DEIA issues were designed and facilitated by Erika G. Bertling. These included 2021 workshops on selfcare and social activism; microaggressions and micro-resistance; racially conscious communication and parenting; and conversations about race. There was also a reading group on a selection of anti-racist readings by James Baldwin, Robin DiAngelo and Oslem Sensoy, and Stacey Abrams. In February 2022, the WCC hosted a pedagogy workshop and panel on teaching race and ethnicity in antiquity.

On the whole, while there have been some institutionally sponsored events, most of the DEIA work in Classics and related fields has been carried out at the grassroots level. Frequently, the impetus for this work comes from individuals or groups of faculty and/or students. This work can be divided into two categories: barriers to access and the amplification of the voices and work of individuals from historically excluded groups.

A major barrier to access for prospective and current students of color studying archaeology is lack of sufficient financial support. This is despite the fact that archaeological fieldwork is an essential component of most archaeology programs and careers. As Laura Heath-Stout and Elizabeth Hannigan have convincingly shown, the scholarships that do exist often do not cover the whole cost of participating in field projects; they 'on average, only cover about half of the cost of field school tuition, not counting lost wages' (Heath-Stout and Hannigan 2020, 127). The financial burden is significantly greater for students in archaeology graduate programs. Although many of these programs provide financial support for their students in the summer, this only partially covers summer expenses. Such expenses frequently include not only airfare, room, and board for fieldwork, but also personal expenses at home, such as rent.

One mutual aid fund has recently made significant strides toward making up the difference. Black Trowel Collective is an organization that, like Sportula Europe, was inspired by the work that The Sportula has been doing for many years. Similar to The Sportula, Black Trowel Collective provides financial support, particularly microgrants, to archaeology students from working-class and historically looted communities. In just a year, the organization distributed over $43,500 to archaeology students in need.[2] The importance of organizations like Black Trowel Collective and their work is underpinned by the fact that students from working-class and historically excluded groups often tend to fall through the cracks left by traditional scholarship programs. However, in recent years, more programs have been developed to cater specifically to the needs of individuals from these groups. Just a few include the Helen Maria Chesnutt Scholarship for Equity in Classical Study (CANE); the Rudolph Masciantonio CAMWS Diversity Award; and the William Sanders Scarborough Fellowship (ASCSA).

A perceived lack of diversity in the field can also be a significant barrier to access. The fact that the fields of Classical Studies and archaeology are overwhelmingly white has already been discussed. This homogeneity is exacerbated when the work of scholars of color is largely ignored. In recent years, the work of these scholars has been amplified more frequently. These initiatives have taken various forms, including conferences, lecture series, newsletters, and blogs. For example, student-led organizations like the London Classicists of Colour have regularly hosted lectures by and panels featuring scholars of color in Classics and related fields.

My own work through *Notes from the Apotheke*, a blog I began in December 2020 about being BIPOC in Classics, has been guided by the same mission of amplifying the voices of scholars from historically excluded groups. In particular, in February 2021, I started a 'BIPOC feature' series to provide a platform for amplifying the voices and work of scholars of color working in Classics and related fields. The posts are written by the guests themselves, and focus on their journey to studying the ancient world, their current work, and their hopes for the future of the field. Since the series began, ten people, including undergraduate and graduate students, faculty members, and independent scholars, have been featured.

Archaeologists of Color in Conversation—A WCC Event

The exposure that my blog gave me paved the way for a recent collaboration with the WCC on a three-part archaeology series. The first installment of the series, which took place in March 2022, aimed to address the experiences of and issues faced by archaeologists of color. In assembling a panel of archaeologists of color (including myself, Dr. Dimitri Nakassis, and Dr. Caroline Cheung), the event contributed to the larger mission of amplifying the voices of individuals from historically excluded backgrounds. The structure of the discussion echoed the three major areas of importance described in the 2021 ESBAA manifesto: recruitment/access; retention/support; and mentorship/allyship. The discussion also aimed to propose actionable steps that individuals, departments, and institutions could take in order to improve access, support, and mentorship for scholars from historically excluded backgrounds. These, as well as the major takeaways from our discussion, are summarized below.

Recruitment/Access

An important takeaway from the roundtable discussion relating to issues of recruitment and access for archaeologists of color concerned fellowships. As mentioned above, more funding opportunities are being created specifically for individuals from historically excluded groups in Classics and related fields. The problem, however, is that these opportunities do not tend to be widely circulated or advertised. This can have serious consequences, particularly, for archaeology students, who may not be aware of scholarships and other opportunities relevant to them (Heath-Stout and Hannigan 2020, 130).

One way to remedy this problem is to be more proactive in bringing these scholarships and other opportunities to the attention of students of color in our departments and institutions. This can be as simple as compiling a list of relevant funds, scholarships, and larger fellowships, pasting it somewhere highly visible and high-trafficked in your department, and/or regularly circulating the list via e-mail. Assuming that any student, but particularly students of color who frequently come from first-generation, low-income, or otherwise non-academic backgrounds, will just know where to look for these opportunities is inequitable.

Retention/Support

In addition to providing more financial support to prospective students of color who want to enter the field, we also need to ensure that the environment in which current students of color work is safe and inclusive. For archaeologists, this notion of creating a habitable professional environment must extend beyond our offices on campus and into our field and lab work as well. Developing our cultural competence is an important first step to making our professional environments more inclusive and supportive.

An important issue that was raised in the discussion during the WCC panel in March 2022 was that, because supervisors are not (usually) trained in cultural competence, they either blow it off or are unable to adequately address such issues when they happen. Cultural competence can be developed in a number of ways, from asking questions of students of color who have worked on projects with you and with whom you have established relationships, to running anonymized surveys at the end of every field season, to attending workshops and lectures. Developing this skill is important and necessary because it enables supervisors and directors of field projects to provide culturally appropriate support to students from backgrounds that are historically underrepresented in archaeology. Culturally competent leadership on field projects is essential to making archaeology more inclusive and supportive, which can lead to better retention overall.

Students, too, can play a proactive role in developing supportive environments for archaeologists of color working on field projects. They can take it upon themselves to ask questions of their peers and of field directors about the (social and cultural) conditions of prospective projects. An important question to consider is whether other students of color have participated before and what their experiences were working there. This approach has been strongly advocated for by Bet Hucks, informed by her own experiences as a Black female archaeologist working regularly in European countries. As Hucks explained, it's best to ask these kinds of questions ahead of time and get the discomfort out of the way, rather than having to learn on the fly, often when it's too late to change your mind.

A final approach to developing supportive environments for archaeologists of color in the field is one involving collaboration between students and faculty. A recent example of a partnership in service of this larger goal is the Behavioral Compact for Field and Laboratory Research developed by the Anti-Racism and Anti-Colonialism (ARCO) community at Cornell University. The topics addressed include accommodations (disability, dietary, and health), cultural norms and expectations, alcohol and controlled substances, discrimination, and how to report any issues of bias or harassment. The authors of these behavioral guidelines stress that it is a living document and should be updated regularly. Indeed, it is likely that not every possible situation will be covered or adequately handled in the field. As concerns arise, documents like the ARCO Behavioral Compact should change to reflect and address those concerns.[3]

Mentorship/Allyship

Since the Black Lives Matter protests in summer 2020, which subsequently spurred many academic departments into thinking more seriously about DEIA work, allyship has been a popular buzzword. Allyship involves thinking and learning about one's own privilege and cultural biases and unlearning harmful ideas and behaviors. Allies commonly engage in reflection, reading, attending workshops, and sharing public statements of solidarity. What allyship lacks, however, are deep, authentic relationships with people in the demographics that are being supported. This is where accomplices come in.

Several authors have considered the relationship between allies and accomplices (Clemens 2017; Powell and Kelly 2017; Harden and Harden-Moore 2019; Watson 2020). The difference between them is simple. Allies may care about social justice issues, but they rarely take action. Flewellyn et al. argue that allies position themselves as 'saviors' or 'undercover agents of the system from which their power flows' (Flewellyn et al. 2021; see also Desnoyers-Colas 2019). By contrast, accomplices show up for the people they support, often using and risking their own privilege to disrupt and interrogate institutional bias.

What might this look like for the field of Mediterranean archaeology? A final recommendation from the WCC roundtable encouraged mentors to facilitate networking for students and early career researchers from historically excluded backgrounds. Mentors should be accomplices, not merely allies. They need to give their mentees a foot in the door by using their own connections and privilege to support them. This means introducing marginalized scholars to other people. It also means talking about and validating the work that they're doing.

Conclusion

Something that I think about often when I consider my position as a Black woman working in the field of ancient Mediterranean archaeology is that it was not until very recently that I became aware of others in this field who looked like me. Of course, they were always out there. Their lack of visibility was simply a by-product of the predominantly white academic environments I was inhabiting.

It is possible that the lack of momentum behind sustained DEIA work in ancient Mediterranean archaeology stems from a lack of comprehensive data on the demographics of the field. As this chapter has shown, much important work in this vein has been and continues to be done at the grassroots level. Facilitating a conversation with archaeologists of color in March 2022 was one way that I have tried to encourage individuals to continue building on this work. Moreover, I believed that highlighting the experiences of archaeologists of color would remind others in the field of how important this work is. But collecting demographic data on the field is something that needs to be done by our larger institutions and professional organizations. Without this data, the experiences, difficulties, and scholarship of archaeologists from historically excluded groups will continue to be overlooked.

Notes

1 SBA, the Columbia Center for Archaeology, and the Theoretical Archaeology Group (2020) 'Archaeology in the Time of Black Lives Matter', Zoom Webinar, https://archaeology.columbia.edu/2020/06/27/video-of-panel-on-archaeology-in-the-time-of-black-lives-matter/, accessed 1 April, 2022.
2 Black Trowel Collective [@BlackTrowel]. 'HAPPY ANNIVERSARY! One year ago today the Black Trowel Collective Microgrants launched. In that time you have helped us distribute an astonishing $43,500 to archaeology students in need. #MutualAid #solidarity', Twitter, 22 June 2021, https://twitter.com/BlackTrowel/status/1407228625548713985, accessed 1 April 2022.
3 ARCO Behavioral Compact for Field and Laboratory Research (2020), https://docs.google.com/document/d/1aKOfLewc8-K4mX5HtBlH25U wRyuGKS6YER70Q0cUcTY/edit#heading=h.poal8vlxvxp3, accessed 3 March 2022.

Works Cited

Abrams, S. (2019) *Lead from the Outside: How to Build Your Future and Make Real Change*, London.

Agbe-Davies, A.S. (2014) *Tobacco, Pipes, and Race in Colonial Virginia: Little Tubes of Mighty Power*, Walnut Creek, CA.

Baldwin, J. (2009 [1963]) 'A Talk to Teachers,' in Why Do We Educate? Voices from the Conversation, ed. M. Smylie. Hoboken: Wiley. 15–20.

Blouin, K. (2017) 'Classical Studies' Glass Ceiling Is White', *Everyday Orientalism*, https://everydayorientalism.wordpress.com/2017/01/10/classical-studies-glass-ceiling-is-white/ (accessed 1 April 2022).

Brunache, P., Dadzie, B.E., Goodlett, K., Hampden, L., Kriescheh, A., Ngonadi, C.V., Parikh, D. and Sires, J.P. (2021) 'Contemporary Archaeology and Anti-Racism: A Manifesto from the European Society of Black and Allied Archaeologists', *European Journal of Archaeology* 24.3: 294–8.

Clancy, K.B.H., Nelson, R.G., Rutherford, J.N. and Hinde, K. (2014) 'Survey of Academic Field Experiences (SAFE): Trainees Report Harassment and Assault', *PloS ONE* 9: e102172.

Clemens, C. (2017) 'Ally or Accomplice? The Language of Activism', *Teaching Tolerance Magazine*, 5 June.

Demery, A.C. and Pipkin, M.A. (2020) 'Safe Fieldwork Strategies for At-Risk Individuals, Their Supervisors and Institutions', *Nature Ecology Evolution* 5: 5–9.

Desnoyers-Colas, E. (2019) 'Talking Loud and Saying Nothing', *Departures in Critical Qualitative Research* 8.4: 100–5.

DiAngelo, R. and Sensoy, O. (2014) 'Calling In: Strategies for Cultivating Humility and Critical Thinking in Antiracism Education', *Understanding and Dismantling Privilege* 4.2: 191–203.

Flewellyn, A.O., Dunnavant, J.P., Odewale, A., Jones, A., Wolde-Michael, T., Crossland, Z. and Franklin, M. (2021) '"The Future of Archaeology Is Antiracist": Archaeology in the Time of Black Lives Matter', *American Antiquity* 86.2: 224–43.

Franklin, M. (1997) 'Why Are There So Few Black American Archaeologists?, *Antiquity* 71: 799–801.

Harden, K. and Harden-Moore, T. (2019) 'Moving from Ally to Accomplice: How Far Are You Willing to Go to Disrupt Racism in the Workplace?', *Diverse Issues in Higher Education*, 36.2.

Heath-Stout, L. and Hannigan, E. (2020) 'Affording Archaeology: How Field School Costs Promote Exclusivity', *Advances in Archaeological Practice* 8.2: 123–33.

Hucks, B. (2021) 'Race, Archaeology and 3D Modeling', hosted by London Classicists of Colour, https://www.youtube.com/watch?v=Gpz4lgKnvEw, accessed 1 April, 2022.

Poser, R. (2021) 'He Wants to Save Classics from Whiteness. Can the Field Survive?' *New York Times*, 2 February.

Powell, J. and Kelly, A. (2017) 'Accomplices in the Academy in the Age of Black Lives Matter', *Journal of Critical Thought and Praxis* 6.2: 42–65.

SCS (2018) 'Harassment and Discrimination Experiences Survey Results Report', Bureau of Sociological Research, University of Nebraska-Lincoln, 1–66, https://classicalstudies.org/sites/default/files/userfiles/files/2018%20SCS%20Survey%20Results%20(1).pdf (accessed 1 April 2022).

Viglione, G. (2020) 'Racism and Harassment Are Common in Field Research—Scientists Are Speaking up', *Nature* 585: 15–16.

Watson, L. (2020) 'Allyship and Accomplice: Two Sides of the Same Coin', *Equity Dispatch* 4.3: 2–8.

White, W. and Draycott, C. (2020) 'Why the Whiteness of Archaeology is a Problem', SAPIENS, https://www.sapiens.org/archaeology/archaeology-diversity/ (accessed 1 April, 2022).

Zeder, M.A. (1997) *The American Archaeologist: A Profile*, Walnut Creek, CA.

3 'Classics Beyond Whiteness'
Race and Antiracism in Departmental Curriculum

T. H. M. Gellar-Goad and Caitlin Hines

The discipline of Classics is in a transitional moment. Perhaps it's a crisis—or, better, an opportunity. In response to growing attention to the histories, legacies, and present impacts of race and racism inside and outside the discipline, some scholars are calling for wholesale reform and reimagining of Classics, with a view toward antiracist and postcolonial possibilities, while others are digging in and calling for retrenchment.[1]

When it comes to reform and reimagining at the level of individual programs, large, R-1 departments are best positioned to lead the charge, such as Princeton Classics with its excellent predoctoral program (see Park 2018). Yet discipline-wide change requires discipline-wide participation, by smaller, less prestigious, and undergraduate-focused institutions as well as the big names. Along those lines, the Department of Classics at Wake Forest University (in Winston-Salem, North Carolina) is, as of the 2021–2022 academic year, the first Classics program anywhere in the world to require all students majoring or minoring in the department to study critical race theory, race and ethnicity in the ancient world, and the history of Classics and white supremacy.

This is, arguably, an unlikely turn of events: the co-authors of this chapter, a professor and a former postdoctoral fellow in the department, are not specialists in these areas, nor are any of our colleagues, and the university is a predominantly white, southern, traditionally Baptist institution with no Classics graduate program and no record of leadership in critical conversations on race and white supremacy. And yet this decision has gained international attention, including an enraged screed in *Le Figaro* (Doan 2021) and a death threat sent to one of the co-authors, T. H. M. Gellar-Goad. The case study we offer here describes how the world-first decision came to pass; what led the university's Classics faculty to embrace inclusivity and diversity in its teaching practices and curricula; and how the department's initiatives

DOI: 10.4324/9781003278016-4

have successfully engaged new audiences in the academic life of the department.

In the 2018–2019 academic year, Gellar-Goad organized a small series of guest lectures at Wake Forest on the theme of 'Classics beyond Europe,' focusing on classical reception outside the conventional geographical bounds of the discipline. Gellar-Goad had been organizing virtual lectures since his arrival at Wake Forest in 2012–2013, long before the advent of COVID-19 and near-universal facility with Zoom, as a way to enliven the intellectual life of a smallish Classics department with an even-more-smallish operating budget. 'Classics beyond Europe' featured lectures from junior and senior scholars across the discipline, and drew more interest from across the campus community than anything the department had seen before, in particular talks by Shelley Haley and Patrice Rankine on race, racism, and the Classics in modern American contexts. Rankine's talk, on race and the idea of 'the commons' in ancient Athens, revolutionary America, and today, was particularly well-timed: arranged before the high-profile racist incidents at the January 2019 Society for Classical Studies conference in San Diego (see Rankine 2019), the talk took place in February 2019, mere days after revelations about Virginia governor Ralph Northam's appearance in racist yearbook photos—and mere days before Wake Forest's own microcosmic version of the Northam scandal, as university librarians uncovered past yearbook photos of high-ranking administrators posing with Confederate flags in their college days. The Wake Forest yearbook photos sparked a sustained antiracist movement on campus led by students and supported by progressive faculty; Rankine's talk had the highest attendance of any Wake Forest Classics event on record up to that point.

In response to this turnout and to on-campus antiracist advocacy energized by similar racist provocations, the co-authors organized a series titled CLASSICS BEYOND WHITENESS for the 2019–2020 academic year.[2] The mission of the series was to examine the misleading and damaging tendency of the field of Classics to center 'whiteness' in its scholarly and educational practices; to chart new paths forward for a more inclusive, constructive vision of the discipline; to celebrate the unique pedagogical, scholarly, and artistic contributions of Black Classicists; to foreground the reception of Classical antiquity by artists and communities of color; to highlight recent efforts to create a more diverse and inclusive field; and to confront the hateful backlash, both online and in professional settings, that has targeted those efforts. The series title was both provocative and aspirational, aiming especially to confront the ugly truth that traditional Classics curricula—what has constituted the core of educational material on antiquity presented to students since the field's foundation—have been and continue to be dominated by attitudes and practices that privilege whiteness.

CLASSICS BEYOND WHITENESS comprised multimedia programming offerings that included guest lectures, workshops, reading groups, film and art exhibitions, the commissioning of a local artist to paint portraits of Black Classicists, and two high-enrollment courses: a general-education course titled Classics Beyond Whiteness, taught by Gellar-Goad, and an advanced Classics seminar titled Ancient Worlds, Modern Crises, taught by Hines.[3] Our goal in designing the series was to be as comprehensive as possible—not just intellectually and formally, but spatially—in order to broadcast how much we lose when we center whiteness: the lack should be felt not just in our classrooms and our lecture halls, but in our hallways, in our libraries, in our theaters, in the books we read, the art we consume, the people we learn from, and the histories we remember. A primary reaction to the series from Wake Forest students was a sense of surprise that there was so much content to be found. This response was felt especially strongly by students of color who affirmed that they had rarely, if ever, seen themselves represented in the discipline, much less in an active or focused way.

A brief summary of the CLASSICS BEYOND WHITENESS events organized for the 2019–2020 academic year will offer a more precise sense of its scope. The series kicked off in early September with a guest lecture by Sarah E. Bond on the use and abuse of ancient history. A reading group on Donna Zuckerberg's *Not All Dead White Men* met biweekly throughout September and October: attendees included students and faculty from a number of disciplines (Religious Studies, Mathematics, English, Women's and Gender Studies, Philosophy, Politics, Divinity) as well as library and administrative staff. Next, E. Ashley Hairston (who happens to be Associate Dean of Advising at Wake Forest and current interim Chair of the Department of Classics) presented his research on classical receptions by Zora Neale Hurston. November began with a dynamic workshop led by Mathura Umachandran on white fragility in Classics, attended by the Provost, the Vice President of Student Life, and the President's chief of staff, in addition to a large student and faculty turnout. The semester concluded with a talk by Jackie Murray on race and the body in Greek and Roman literature.

Behind the scenes of this fall programming, the co-organizers were appealing to numerous grant sources in order to obtain enough funding to commission Winston-Salem artist Leo Rucker to paint three large portraits of Black Classicists from North Carolina: Helen Maria

Chesnutt, Charlotte Hawkins Brown, and Wiley Lane. The first of these portraits was formally unveiled at the start of the spring semester, at a reception to kick off the 14 Black Classicists art exhibition which would be on display throughout the spring in a much-used reading room in the WFU Library. This traveling exhibition features the images and biographies of Black scholars, teachers, and leaders in the field of Classics whose forgotten histories have been recovered by the archival research of Michele Valerie Ronnick (see Ronnick 2004; Eisen 2018). February's offering was a screening and expert panel discussion of Spike Lee's problematic modern take on the *Lysistrata* story, *Chi-raq*. In March, Dani Bostick spoke about the erasure of oppression as a weapon of white supremacy in Classics, especially in pedagogical materials designed for primary school students.[4]

As complement to these extracurricular offerings, the co-organizers designed and taught original courses keyed to the principles of antiracist and inclusive pedagogy.[5] The first of these courses, Classics Beyond Whiteness, designed and taught by Gellar-Goad, was a half-term course that met no requirements besides elective credit for Classical Studies majors and minors, yet overenrolled with one of the most diverse cohorts the department has ever seen.[6] The course followed three threads of inquiry: race and ethnicity in the ancient Greek and Roman worlds; Classics and modern racial politics, including white supremacy; and non-white classical reception. Class sessions focused on learner-centered activities including a variety of discussion formats (see, e.g., Gonzalez 2015), respectful but honest debate, and intersectional thinking. The key textbook for the course was McCoskey 2012, along with articles from a variety of internet sources, especially *Eidolon*.

The second course, titled Ancient Worlds, Modern Crises[7] and designed and taught by Hines, offered students the chance to critically examine ancient and modern texts in dialogue with each other and invited them to respond actively and creatively to this material. One principle foundational to the course design was the destabilization of supposedly authoritative truths about the ancient world and its relationship to the modern world: students spent the first day of the course deconstructing the terms 'Western civilization,' 'scholarly objectivity,' and even 'Classics' itself. Students were encouraged throughout the term to complicate notions of primacy and unidirectionality in thinking through the relationships between ancient and modern texts—that is, to consider not just how the ancient texts provide source material for the modern, but also how the modern materials can inform, enrich, and even transform our understanding of the ancient ones.

The course progressed through six modules graded according to a specifications model, offering students transparency and control over the grade they were working to earn. Module 1 on Homer and War Trauma combined readings from the *Iliad* with Jonathan Shay's *Achilles in Vietnam* to examine, first, how ancient epic can be a useful tool for veterans to process the traumatic experiences of combat, and, second, how the perspectives of modern veterans shed valuable light in return on the epics themselves. In Module 2, the students read *Antigone* alongside *The Island,* a play by Athol Fugard, John Kani, and Winston Ntshona that tells the story of two South African men incarcerated on an island (modeled after Robben Island) rehearsing and performing a two-man production of *Antigone*. Module 3 presented Aristophanes' *Lysistrata* alongside Spike Lee's *Chi-raq* (the film screening and panel discussion mentioned above coordinated with this unit in the course schedule); Module 4 had the students reading Ovid's *Ars Amatoria* in light of the modern 'Pick-Up Artist' and 'red pill' communities' uncritical usage of the work to justify misogyny, sexual harassment, and assault (Zuckerberg 2018, 89–142); Module 5 turned to material culture and antiquities theft, encouraging the students to analyze the Parthenon first as an architectural and artistic achievement, and next in terms of competing claims to ownership over the Parthenon Marbles; Module 6 focused on death and music via the myth of Orpheus and its adaptations into the popular Broadway production *Hadestown* and the ballet choreographed by Pina Bausch to Gluck's 'Orpheus and Eurydice.'

Coursework for each Module in Ancient Worlds, Modern Crises featured a combination of analytical writing and creative production. The shape of the writing assignments was directed by a series of prompts about the module's primary materials; no restrictions were placed on the scope, medium, or mode of presentation for the creative responses beyond a specified minimum for time spent in conceiving and producing the project and an accompanying commentary explaining creative choices in connection with the primary materials. The range of creative receptions produced during this semester went far beyond what the instructor ever imagined: there were original poems, songs, artworks, and critical essays, but also YouTube videos and TikToks, course syllabi, lecture series, Twitter accounts, podcasts, and even an entire play. Students' enthusiasm for these assignments was evident in their length and scope, which went far beyond expectations. The course used specifications grading (see Nilson 2014), which meant that each individual component needed only to pass a minimum standard for credit; higher grades were achieved by the quantity of works submitted to meet the specified standards. For this reason, the extraordinary efforts that went into these creative responses should be attributed more to enthusiasm than to grade anxiety. One final requirement applied to each of these creative responses: the students had to think carefully about their language, their methods, and their audience with a particular aim to do no harm; as much of the analytical thrust of course discussions ended up revolving around the accidental harm that can be done even by those with good intentions, students were especially careful to anticipate the impact of their creative choices, to consider whose voices they might be unintentionally excluding, suppressing, or undercutting, and to revise their designs accordingly.

Since Ancient Worlds, Modern Crises met in the spring semester, the COVID-19 pandemic posed a number of obstacles to the course as originally planned, which included not only the unplanned transition to online instruction but also a problem of time zones. It is a testament to the commitment of the students—but perhaps also to their genuine interest in the course content—that even with the option to work asynchronously all of them continued attending class live, some of them logging on to Zoom as early as 6:30 am in their local time zones. Even with the awkwardness and unfamiliarity of online platforms, the discussion was lively, honest, and respectful. Perhaps because of the course's established interest in connecting readings to the modern world, students began (without the instructor's prompting) to use the ancient material to process the present trauma of the pandemic. As the risk of infection prevented many Americans from arranging traditional funerals for their loved ones, they reached back to *Antigone* to think through the private and social pain of being unable to perform cultural rituals for the dead. As resistance to government policies on social distancing and masking began to spread, students returned to *Lysistrata* to think through the cultural contours of protest and to examine what degree of responsibility citizens should have for the safety of others in their community. The concluding module on death and music was perhaps more somber than the instructor had intended, especially as worldwide forecasts for pandemic-related deaths grew ever more dire and distressing, but it was also extremely poignant, as students used the story of Orpheus and Eurydice to explore questions about the persistence of love beyond death and the healing power of music.

The CLASSICS BEYOND WHITENESS series also proved timely in tragic ways, as 2020's summer of racial-justice protests sparked by police murders of Tony McDade, Breonna Taylor, George Floyd, and others bore out. The efforts of student and faculty antiracist organizers at Wake Forest, and the mass social movements and global activist uprising of 2020, pushed the university to issue calls for and claims of commitment to greater equity. At the same time, a group of Wake Forest Classics alums wrote a letter to the department that encouraged department faculty to increase our own efforts still further.[8] In response to these calls from within and outside the university to take action on antiracist initiatives, the faculty committed the Department to embed antiracist pedagogy in all of its courses, and furthermore—in order to address the alums' exhortation to make sure that no student came through our department without encountering critical race theory—we voted to make the Classics Beyond Whiteness course a requirement for every student pursuing a degree in the department, whether as a major or minor, whether focused on language or on culture. That curriculum change was approved by the college-wide faculty in February 2021 and has taken effect for all newly declared majors and minors as of the fall 2022 semester.

The CLASSICS BEYOND WHITENESS series continues, though in-person restrictions and budgetary privations of the COVID-19 pandemic have necessarily diminished the extent of the programming, as well as its reach and engagement. Still, the Classics Department has continued to host talks and reading groups under this rubric, and the 2021–2022 academic year kicked off with a celebration of the installation of Leo Rucker's three portraits of Black Classicists from North Carolina in their permanent home on the hallway where most Classics courses are held.

CLASSICS BEYOND WHITENESS and the curricular reforms that it has inspired are responsible for another important development for Wake Forest Classics. In the 2021–2022 academic year, the Dean of Wake Forest College authorized a brand-new tenure-line hire for a Classics faculty member whose agenda substantially includes race, racism, and Greek and Roman studies. We believe the Dean's decision was informed by a combination of factors: good enrollments across departmental courses, continued departmental commitment to teaching in-demand general-education courses, the department's global leadership within the discipline in making Classics Beyond Whiteness a requirement, and local, engaged activity at Wake Forest and in Winston-Salem. This new hire, starting July 2023, will be the first such specialist to hold a professorship in Classics at Wake Forest University, will teach the Classics Beyond Whiteness course in alternation with Gellar-Goad, will help build the CLASSICS BEYOND WHITENESS series, and will reify the department's long-term commitment to equity and inclusive teaching, mentoring, and collegiality.

We close this case study with some practical advice for advocates interested in replicating or adapting the successes of Wake Forest University's Department of Classics. First and foremost, start small but think big. CLASSICS BEYOND WHITENESS began essentially as a simple extension of 'Classics Beyond Europe,' which itself originated as a theme used to select the specific slate of speakers for one year of an ongoing lecture series. And the two of us came up with what turned out to be the core of CLASSICS BEYOND WHITENESS by taking a walk and thinking 'blue sky': what could we do if cost wasn't an object? This combination of incremental innovations on preexisting structures and optimistic brainstorming helped us organize a vision that was feasible, actionable, and fundable. The department's decision to make the Classics Beyond Whiteness course a major/minor requirement was likewise both incremental and wildly optimistic. On the incremental side: Gellar-Goad put together a half-term course to match the series after it had been conceived and then got it put on the books as a permanent, full-term course, which, in turn, was immediately to hand when department faculty were discussing the action item of putting all students in our department into contact with critical race theory. On the wildly optimistic side: we took a plunge without a model at any other Classics program and without being certain that we would secure support either from the college-wide faculty for such a new, immediately relevant requirement or from the Dean's office for the staffing of that course requirement.

Second, plan collaboratively and grantseek comprehensively. Neither of us alone could have managed to build a series as packed with events as the 2019–2020 academic year was. The process, from brainstorming to execution, was richer, more creative, more productive, and more successful because we worked together at each step. When it came to finding funding, we left no stone unturned and paired grant sources together to increase their impact. Modest support authorized by our department chair allowed us to secure similarly modest funding from the Wake Forest University Office of Diversity and Inclusion and the Classical Association of the Middle West and South; put together, these funds were not so modest and could stand as matching funds for larger grants both internal (from the Provost's office) and external (from the Society for Classical Studies). We pulled on our networks at the university to get support for specific portions of the series from the library and from student government, and across the discipline to find the right speakers and right programming choices—including, for instance, a free e-visit from Donna Zuckerberg for a meeting of the reading group on her book.

The title of this chapter speaks of 'Curriculum,' but we want to emphasize also the significance of what is *extra*curricular, both in terms of program offerings outside the structures of traditional coursework and in terms of the spaces occupied by our students. When it comes to departmental programming, the extracurricular *is* curricular, and larger-scale academic paradigm shifts can and should start outside the classroom. The turnout and positive response to CLASSICS BEYOND WHITENESS is what helped persuade skeptical colleagues and administrators that there was demand for the study of Classics at Wake Forest and the study of race, racism, white supremacy, and reform within the study of Classics at Wake Forest. The speakers we invite into our (physical or digital) lecture halls, the portraits we choose to hang on our walls, and the works we center when we expand our reach beyond Classics-specific spaces all model for our students what, and whom, we value.

Finally, don't be afraid to go for it, even—especially—if you don't feel ready. Neither of us came into the CLASSICS BEYOND WHITENESS project with teaching experience or graduate training or a publication record on race in antiquity, Classics and modern racial politics, or non-white reception and practice of Classics. But there are great people out there doing amazing work on it, and they are almost all of them generous, high-minded, and eager to share their expertise and perspectives. (Make sure not to exploit their generosity: fair wages for intellectual labor were a bedrock principle for us in organizing the series.) These topics are no more difficult to get acquainted with than any other subfield of Classics, and they should be a lot less mysterious than many subfields, especially given their crucial place in the current trajectory of the discipline and as one of the predominant intellectual-political discourses in the world at this moment. Large-scale overhauls are not the only way you can get yourself and your department involved in charting a new path forward for the discipline, and every change and improvement you make will better your university community and make your classrooms and hallways more inclusive. This is worth your time.

Notes

1 In the first category, among numerous leading voices, we name (in alphabetical order by last name) Dani Bostick, Sasha-Mae Eccleston, Shelley Haley, Nandini Pandey, Dan-el Padilla Peralta, Patrice Rankine, and Mathura Umachandran. The second category is represented not only by atavistic cultural commentary in media outlets such as *The New Criterion* and *Quilette*, but also backwards-moving, yesteryear-nostalgic assessments of the discipline such as Adler (2020).

2 Earlier coverage of CLASSICS BEYOND WHITENESS includes McGrath (2020) and Lather (2021).
3 A comprehensive programming list can be accessed at https://classics.wfu.edu/fall-2019-spring-2020-classics-beyond-whiteness-events.
4 In mid-March of 2020, the start of the COVID-19 pandemic and unexpected move to online instruction led to the cancellation of those events meant to conclude the series. This change of plans, though disappointing in the short-term, turned out to be an interruption rather than a decisive conclusion, as students expressed continued interest in the series' mission even after the academic year ended. As with many academic activities in 2020, CLASSICS BEYOND WHITENESS transformed, after a brief hiatus, into a virtual series, and then into a hybrid offering after students were permitted to return to campus.
5 Seminal scholarship establishing these principles includes hooks (1994); Haley (2009); and Kendi (2019). For a great starting point, check out the reading list compiled by Aebersold: https://dtei.uci.edu/antiracist-pedagogy-reading-list/.
6 The course had 27 students, a majority of whom were students of color, coming both from the Classics department and across the College (including majors in Sociology, History, and elsewhere, in addition to as-yet-undeclared first- and second-year students). For a point of comparison on enrollment numbers, general-education literature courses at Wake Forest tend to range from 16 students (in English) to 25 (in Classics). The enrollment in Classics Beyond Whiteness was limited by chairs and space available in its assigned classroom.
7 Inspired by the title of this course, the Society for Classical Studies 'Classics Everywhere' Initiative—from which we received grant funding for the Classics beyond Whiteness series and by which CLASSICS BEYOND WHITENESS was featured on the SCS Blog (Papathanasopoulou 2019)—has since changed its name to 'Ancient Worlds, Modern Communities.' Like the Classics Beyond Whiteness course, Ancient Worlds, Modern Crises had high enrollment: 12 students in a seminar-level class, higher than average for Wake Forest Classics.
8 This letter was inspired by the urgent and insistent demands for change in similar letters sent by current and former graduate students to the Classics programs at Oxford University and Bryn Mawr College.

Works Cited

Adler, E. (2020) *The Battle of the Classics: How a Nineteenth-Century Debate Can Save the Humanities Today*, Oxford.

Doan, R. (2021) 'Ces Historiens De l'Antiquité Qui Haissent l'Antiquité', *FigaroVox*, 11 March.

Eisen, E. (2018) 'Hidden Figures: The Importance of Remembering Black Classicists', *The Guardian*, 4 June.

Gonzalez, J. (2015) 'The Big List of Class Discussion Strategies', *Cult of Pedagogy*, 15 October.

Haley, S.P. (2009) 'Be Not Afraid of the Dark: Critical Race Theory and Classical Studies', in L. Nasrallah and E.S. Fiorenza (eds.), *Prejudice and Christian Beginnings*, Minneapolis, 27–50.

hooks, b. (1994) *Teaching to Transgress: Education as the Practice of Freedom*, London.
Kendi, I.X. (2019) *How to Be an Antiracist*, New York, NY.
Lather, A. (2021) 'Classics Beyond Whiteness: An Interview', *Sententiae Antiquae*, 9 March.
McCoskey, D.E. (2012) *Race: Antiquity and Its Legacy*, London.
McGrath, K. (2020) '"Classics Beyond Whiteness": Relevant, inclusive', *Wake Forest News*, 7 February.
Nilson, L.B. (2014) *Specifications Grading: Restoring Rigor, Motivating Students, and Saving Faculty Time*, Sterling, VA.
Papathanasopoulou, N. (2019) 'Classics Everywhere: Examining the Past with a Comparative and Critical Eye', *SCS Blog*. https://classicalstudies.org/scs-blog/nina-papathanasopoulou/blog-classics-everywhere-examining-past-comparative-and-critical-eye
Park, A. (2018) 'Diversifying Classics: A New Initiative at Princeton', SCS Blog, https://classicalstudies.org/scs-blog/arum-park/blog-diversifying-classics-new-initiative-princeton
Rankine, P.D. (2019) 'The Classics, Race, and Community-Engaged or Public Scholarship', *American Journal of Philology* 140.2: 345–59.
Ronnick, M.V. (2004) 'Twelve Black Classicists', *Arion* 11.3: 85–102.
Zuckerberg, D. (2018) *Not All Dead White Men*, Cambridge, MA.

4 Race, Roman Law Courts, and the Colonized Subject

Teaching Cicero's *Pro Fonteio*

Denise Eileen McCoskey

Introduction

In 69 B.C.E., the Roman orator Marcus Tullius Cicero defended a former governor of Transalpine Gaul, Marcus Fonteius, against charges of extortion. Marcus Fonteius, who had held the position from around 74 to 72 B.C.E. (Dyck 2012, 12), was being tried in the court for officials accused of misconduct in the provinces, the *quaestio de repetundis*, which had been founded in 149 B.C.E. and was the oldest standing court in Rome (Dyck 2012, 2). For unknown reasons, the case had been adjourned for a time and Cicero's speech, the *Pro Fonteio*, seemingly comes from the second hearing. The *Pro Fonteio* is our only evidence for the trial and it suggests that Fonteius was primarily accused of allowing the province to fall into enormous debt, presumably to his own financial benefit (ch. 11); other charges included that he accepted bribes in connection with major road work (ch. 17–18) and created a new duty on wine (ch. 19–20).[1] While the outcome of the trial is not preserved, it is generally assumed that Fonteius was acquitted since Cicero records in a later letter that he bought an expensive house in Naples (Dyck 2012, 15; Cicero, *ad Att.* 1.6).

Speeches like Cicero's *Pro Fonteio* provide invaluable evidence of Rome's conduct of its early empire, but they can be daunting sources for non-specialists and students. Nonetheless, I have had success incorporating the *Pro Fonteio* into my undergraduate course on race and ethnicity in antiquity. This class, which can be used to satisfy a requirement for either the Classical Studies or Critical Race and Ethnic Studies major at my university, or taken as a general elective, generally has an enrollment of both White students and students of color. Although my students have widely varying perspectives and training upon entering the class, if they are provided with sufficient background and frameworks for analysis, which I would like to share here, they can grapple skillfully with the role of race in Cicero's speech and also apply what they have learned to analysis of some of the racialized institutions and ideologies that structure their own lives.

As Frantz Fanon has asserted, 'The colonist and colonized are old acquaintances. And consequently, the colonist is right when he says he "knows" them. It is the colonist who *fabricated* and *continues to fabricate* the colonized subject' (2004, 2).[2] Cicero's *Pro Fonteio* falls within a long tradition of Roman texts that present the 'Gauls' as a distinct racial group, one that is inherently dangerous, unruly, and the very antithesis of virtuous Roman colonists. Cicero's speech, however, does not merely record pre-existing racial stereotypes; it also reshapes and further disseminates them, providing ample illustration of Fanon's assertion that the colonist's act of fabricating the colonized subject is invariably an ongoing project. Like many Roman authors, Cicero characterizes Gallic identity as both categorically different from that of the Romans and unchanging over time. Yet this strategy defies the fact that, over the centuries, the Gauls were forced to respond to Rome's shifting strategies of violence and material exploitation—contexts and circumstances that Cicero is forced to admit in other parts of his speech. Thus, Cicero's speech presents a welcome opportunity for both unpacking the Roman racial construction of the 'Gauls' and for identifying some of the concrete political and economic structures that circumscribed the formation of colonial identities in the first half of the first century B.C.E.

Who Were the 'Gauls'?

It has become routine to characterize race as a social construction, a form of identity that derives from ideas about human variation that are dependent on time and place. Race is, therefore, best perceived not as a static or innate quality, but rather as a *process* by which an identity, generally premised on select features (such as skin color in the modern world), is attributed or imposed onto others and/or claimed or performed by oneself. Moreover, although race stems primarily from a set of mental activities—from ideas about what makes groups distinct and why—it can acquire its own material reality when such ideas are mobilized, for example, when the impulse for defining racial groups leads to the unequal distribution of resources or even direct violence. Most students today are fairly comfortable with the designation of race as a social construction, but the case of the Gauls nonetheless presents students with an invaluable demonstration of this principle given the contingencies and uncertainties that attended the emergence and operation of 'Gaul' as a racial category in antiquity.

'Gauls' (*Galli* or *Galatae*) was a term primarily employed by the Romans, and the 'Gauls' were often equated with the 'Celts' (from the Greek *Keltoi*), a group that first appeared in the work of Hecataeus of Miletus in the late sixth century B.C.E. (Dietler 1994, 585). Both terms seem to denote peoples living in northwestern Europe, although the Romans themselves were often uncertain about the parameters of their label, including when it came to drawing spatial and conceptual boundaries between Gauls and the neighboring Germans (Murdoch 2004, 60; see also Wells 1995).[3] To modern scholars, the validity of treating people in that area as a single group has often seemed supported by the fact that the archaeological record of Iron Age communities in northwestern Europe shows 'considerable similarity over wide regions' (Dietler 1994, 586), a shared assemblage often called 'La Tène' (e.g., Wells 1995). However, Michael Dietler (1994, 586) has argued that it is more accurate to conceive of this region as housing, not a single 'Celtic culture' but rather 'a fluid network of autonomous 'societies, exhibiting considerable' variation in political organization and other sociocultural structures and practices resulting from local trajectories of historical development.'[4] Dietler's emphasis on local variation underlines the fact that homogenizing labels like 'Gaul' and 'Celt', imposed by outsiders, presumably bore little relation to the ways people in that part of the world self-identified. Indeed, even as they enthusiastically trafficked in broad stereotypes, many Roman writers clearly knew enough about the space they considered 'Gaul' to reference the names of individual communities living there; there is accordingly a tension between the manufacture of a generic Gaul in Roman ethnography and art and the discussion in Roman historical accounts of actions taken by specific groups in Gaul, such as the Saluvii and Vocontii.

A range of qualities was traditionally assigned to the Gauls in Roman racial discourse, such as the possession of large, powerful bodies and the habit of drinking to excess.[5] As Greg Woolf (2011, 23) has noted, the designation of these specific features can be traced in large part to the fact that the idea of the 'Gaul' was formed primarily in relation to their perceived and ongoing threat to Roman observers. So, too, such stereotypes remained remarkably impervious to change, even as historical contexts were radically shifting (Woolf 2011, 112), especially throughout the Roman era. Yet it is precisely because context is so often obscured in Rome's depictions of its colonized subjects that I try to make it visible to my students when studying Cicero's speech. Meaning that while it is important for students to examine *how* 'Gauls' are constructed as a racial group in texts like the *Pro Fonteio*,

I also ask them to take into account Rome's history of intervention in Gaul so they can examine *why* and *under what conditions* such a racial category was produced and reproduced.

The Roman 'Conquest' of Gaul

Around 390 B.C.E., the so-called Gauls sacked the city of Rome, an act that was 'in a sense, the start of modern Roman history for the authors of the late Republic' (Williams 2001, 140). Even as Rome would rebuild and embark on centuries of war and expansion, the trauma of this event occupied a prominent place in Roman memory and cast a long shadow on Roman perceptions of the Gauls. The subsequent Roman conquest of Gaul, in turn, was ongoing and often inconclusive. As Woolf (1998, 32) phrases it, 'The point is not that the Gauls were not conquered and pacified—they were repeatedly—but rather that the establishment of a Roman order *(pax)* in Gaul was a longer process than Romans liked to admit.' By the 190s, the peoples south of the Alps in what is today northern Italy (known as Cisalpine Gaul or Gallia Togata) had been brutally subdued by the Romans. They would subsequently acquire Latin rights around 89 B.C.E. and Roman citizenship in 49 B.C.E. (Häussler 2013, 36–7); notably, the former event pre-dates Cicero's speech by approximately two decades. In further illustration of the considerable gap between Cicero's hostile stereotype of the 'Gauls' and the myriad ways people in different parts of Gaul were actually incorporated into the empire over time, it is useful to remind students that both Catullus (b. 84 B.C.E.) and Vergil (b. 70 B.C.E.) were born in Cisalpine Gaul.

The province of Transalpine Gaul (often simply called 'Province' by the Romans or, later, Gallia Narbonensis) covered the southern part of Gaul along the Mediterranean and was acquired by the Romans around 121 B.C.E. Unlike territories further inland, this region had long been connected to other parts of the Mediterranean by trade, especially following the foundation of the colony of Massilia (Massalia in Greek and, today, Marseille) by Greek settlers from the city of Phocaea around 600 B.C.E. Massilia became an important ally of Rome in the centuries following (Dietler 2010, 122; Dyck 2012, 9); in fact, the Roman presence that eventually led to conquest had been initiated by a request from Massilia for aid (Dietler 2010, 7). Rome's intervention was soon followed by the construction of a road linking Italy and Spain, the Via Domitia, as well as the foundation in 118 B.C.E. of a colony called Narbo Martius (Woolf 1998, 38), whose special status can be seen in Cicero's speech. Rome's early interest in

Transalpine Gaul hinged on its role as a market for Roman exports in wine and its access to Spain (Dyck 2012, 10), where Pompey was waging a major war from 77 to 71 B.C.E. Still, the Romans were required to deal with both invasions and internal uprisings in Transalpine Gaul for decades, an instability alluded to in Cicero's speech (Dietler 2010, 125-6).

Approximately ten years after Cicero's *Pro Fonteio*, Julius Caesar used Transalpine Gaul as the launching point for a series of campaigns lasting from 58-51 B.C.E. in the interior of Gaul, a region often called Gallia Comata (or 'long-haired Gaul'). Caesar's actions initiated centuries of dramatic political and cultural transformations in Gaul, as would the later measures undertaken by Augustus (Woolf 1998, 38-9). The overall violence of this process should not be underestimated; Maria Wyke, for one, has asserted that Caesar's campaigns 'resulted in devastating genocide and the slow destruction of a sophisticated Celtic civilization' (Wyke 2008, 46). Although outside consideration of Cicero's speech, the Romans would eventually establish three additional provinces in the northern parts of Gaul (Lugdunensis, Aquitania, and Belgica); notably, two future emperors, Claudius and Caracalla, were born in Lugdunum (today, Lyon) in Gallia Lugdunensis.[6]

While an understanding of Gaul's history is important to understanding the *Pro Fonteio*, it is also useful, by way of giving context to the speech, to introduce students to Cicero's life and status as a Roman author, including what he himself may have thought about, and contributed to, Rome's imperial project.

Cicero as Imperial Author

Cicero was born in 106 B.C.E. in Arpinum in central Italy; while his family was generally well-off, none of its members had ever previously held a major office at Rome, making him a 'new man' (a *novus homo*) or political outsider. After moving to Rome, Cicero gained extensive training in oratory and philosophy, also serving in the military briefly during the Social Wars. His first published speech was given in 81 B.C.E.,[7] but following a successful defense of Roscius, which may have set the dictator Sulla against him (May 2002, 5), Cicero set off on lengthy travels in Greece and Asia Minor. Two years later, he returned to Rome and began his political career, serving as a quaestor (a type of financial officer) in Sicily in 75 B.C.E. In 70 B.C.E., he was asked to prosecute Verres, the governor of Sicily, for extortion and Cicero's winning prosecution made him 'one of Rome's premier public speakers' (May 2002, 6). His speech on behalf of Fonteius is generally dated to the following year.[8]

Students do not need to master the ins and outs of Cicero's career in the years following, although they are often shocked to learn that he was himself a casualty of Rome's civil wars in 43 B.C.E. Perhaps most relevant to discussion of the *Pro Fonteio* is the fact that Cicero—whose relationships with members of the powerful triumvirate of Pompey, Caesar, and Crassus would ebb and flow—delivered an enthusiastic endorsement of Caesar's request to continue his campaigns in the interior of Gaul *(de provinciis consularibus)*.[9] Cicero's support for Caesar's extra-legal activities seems to many scholars inconsistent with his reputation for defending traditional Republican political structures (Steel 2001, 114). Similarly, the juxtaposition of Cicero's prosecution of Verres with his defense of Fonteius has suggested to some a patent contradiction (Ward 1968, 802).

Yet Cicero's precise attitudes toward Rome's territorial expansion can be difficult to pin down. In a much-cited letter (dated to 60 B.C.E.), Cicero presumes to offer lengthy advice about the duties of a provincial governor to his brother Quintus, who had been serving as governor of Asia, encouraging him to be prudent and self-disciplined, while also warning him of the abuses that might be attempted by other Roman officials and businesspeople around him (QFr.1.1). C. E. W. Steel has proposed that, in Cicero's speeches, much like in the letter to his brother, Cicero narrowly framed 'the problems which arise in the running of empire … as the result of personal failings rather than endemic to the structures of government' (Steel 2001, 4). Moreover, this approach allowed him 'to avoid having to make public choices about the exploitation of imperial resources which could alienate many of his supporters' (4). The notion that Cicero was more concerned with weighing the merits of individual actors and consolidating personal relationships than adjudicating structures of exploitation *per se* resonates with the argument made by some that Cicero both prosecuted Verres and defended Fonteius in order to gain the support of Pompey (Ward 1968, 802–3).[10]

Yet allowing students to interpret Cicero's public pronouncements about empire as solely a matter of opportunism or political expediency can be too simplistic, and Peter Rose (1995) has argued that inconsistencies in Cicero's treatment point 'to the contradictions of Roman society itself as a "system"' (386). Thus, regardless of Cicero's 'personal antipathies and preferences' (389), Rose posits that Cicero 'saw very clearly the impossibly contradictory character of a rule that claimed to seek the best interests of all while being based upon the systemic exploitation of the vast majority' (373–4). In this way, students need not 'resolve' every contradiction they find in the *Pro Fonteio*—the mere identification of such moments can allow them to reflect on the self-contradictory nature of empire itself. Rose ultimately deems Cicero 'complicitous' in these contradictions (397), and this assertion, too, can generate discussion of the ways writers like Cicero are directly involved in shaping the meaning and conduct of colonial projects, not least when providing justifications for them.[11]

The part of the *Pro Fonteio* that most provokes my students, however, is Cicero's argument that the Gauls cannot be trusted to provide credible testimony in Roman courts because of how badly they have been treated under Roman rule, which has led them to impassioned identification of parallels in both law and society today. But in order to prepare for these types of comparisons, I ask my students first to analyze in greater depth Cicero's representation of the human participants enmeshed in Rome's imperial system.

Mapping the Colonized and Colonist

In analyzing Cicero's fabrication of the 'Gauls' as a distinct racial group, it is important for students to grapple with both his methods and his outcomes—what the category of 'Gaul' signifies in Cicero's work and the structures of argument he uses to get there.[12] In the latter case, perhaps most importantly, Cicero follows general Roman practice by framing the positions of colonist and colonized as binary oppositions.[13] Such a strategy is patently obvious in the conclusion of his speech as he weighs what is allegedly involved for the Roman jury in deciding the case (49), but students should be asked to identify this method in other places (e.g., 4), including passages where the opposing group is merely implied. So, too, students should track Cicero's frequent use of the collective term 'Gaul' in producing a homogenous and ahistorical racial category (conversely, he names individual Gallic groups only rarely to provoke derision, 26)[14]—a clear contrast to the specificity he gives to those on the Roman side, who are distinguished by name, occupation, and, at times, social class.

In building his profile of the 'Gauls' as a racial group, Cicero sprinkles negative assessments throughout the speech, with features such as 'avaricious' (21) or 'angry' and 'impious' (15)—presented as essential qualities rather than merely circumstantial. Ancient views of racial difference notably did not prioritize skin color differences, and Cicero evokes both general 'character' traits and various forms of social practice in defining the Gauls for his audience.[15] Addressing their physical presence in Rome, for example, he calls attention to their disorderly forms of clothing (trousers!), demeanor (arrogance rather than modesty), and language (equating the speaking of their own language with making threats) (33). At one point, Cicero dramatically names what he considers the most fundamental difference between the Gauls and other nations: their lack of reverence for the gods, an accusation that culminates in his 'reminder' that the Gauls practice human sacrifice (31).[16]

While many of these ideas draw on the general Roman stereotype of Gauls, Cicero persistently highlights the consequences Gallic 'character' has for their participation in court; their lack of piety, for one, means they do not have the appropriate respect for oaths (30). Even more, he accuses Indutiomarus, the only Gaul he names (46), of arrogance because he frames his testimony as what he 'knows' rather than 'thinks'—the latter a verb Cicero insists is used by everyone else to show appropriate humility (29). Not content to insinuate the Gauls' fundamental incompatibility with the operation of the Roman courtroom, Cicero further claims that they threaten violence if Fonteius is acquitted (33), i.e., that they will not abide by the jury's decision, and so are perverting the very purpose of the courtroom by using it as another means of continuing their war against the Romans (e.g., 44).

In crafting the opposing category of 'Roman colonist', Cicero markedly shifts his strategies, presenting the Roman side as an incarnation of the empire itself. Those allegedly standing ready to support Fonteius, thus, reiterate Rome's geographic reach, including both the provinces of Macedonia and Spain (where Fonteius had served as legate) and individual 'pro-Roman' sites within Gaul, specifically the 'colonists' in Narbo (i.e., Narbo Martius) and 'allies' in Massilia (13 and 14–15).[17] So, too, Cicero provides a fawning account of Fonteius himself, praising his qualities (37–40) and then claiming that Rome needs men like Fonteius, especially since they are no longer easy to find (42–3). Cicero likewise commends Fonteius' family background (41), pointing out to great rhetorical effect his female relatives allegedly sitting in the courtroom, including his Vestal Virgin sister (46–8).

While Cicero often alludes to what Romans *are* as opposed to Gauls, referencing, for example, Fonteius' 'virtue' in close juxtaposition with Gallic 'anger' and 'disloyalty' (15–16), he more often identifies Fonteius' Roman supporters through their status and occupation, what they *do*, underlining the range of individuals who served Rome's interests (as well as their own) in the provinces. While he perhaps unsurprisingly claims that members of the military (16) are allegedly standing on Fonteius' side, Cicero even more frequently cites the support of tax collectors, farmers, and other businessmen (46; cf. 11–12), thereby highlighting the economic dimensions of Rome's imperial project. As Andrew Dyck (2012, 10) writes, following the foundation of Narbo Martius, '(o)ther Romans followed in the colonists' wake to serve their needs and to exploit emerging business opportunities', and these private individuals were key in making the transition from Roman conquest to Roman rule; so deeply rooted did they become that, as Cicero boasts, '(n)ot one of the Gauls conducts any business without a Roman citizen' (11; see also Woolf 1998, 45–6). In all, as Cicero insinuates, it is their very support for, and embeddedness in, the colonial system that ensures the credibility of Fonteius' allies in the Roman courtroom.

As the fundamental differences between 'Gauls' and 'Romans' become clearer, then, it is evident that to be a Gaul, in Cicero's eyes, is to be divorced from place, except in the broadest sense—their hometowns in Gaul are left unnamed, even as they are presented as fundamentally 'alien' in both the courtroom and city of Rome itself—and to exist outside the daily economic activities and family structures that define the Romans. Even more, Cicero emphasizes that time is a factor that has worked progressively against the Gauls, reminding the jury that although the Gauls have engaged in 'bitter and long-lasting' wars with the Roman people, they are now conquered by Rome, humiliated in 'triumphs and monuments', and 'stripped of their lands and cities' (12). As this account of their current status suggests, Cicero at times cuts against the universalizing stereotypes that paint the Gauls as dangerous by nature and instead references what has been done to them, thereby allowing students to apprehend some of the coercive practices and systems underlying Rome's provincial administration.

Identifying Imperial Structures

One of the most surprising parts of the *Pro Fonteio* for my students is Cicero's open admission of the routine exploitation the Gauls have experienced; far from treating such oppression as atypical or something to be condemned, Cicero uses it merely to explain why they cannot be trusted. In the course of his speech, Cicero defines the Gauls again and again by what has been seized from them, and I ask my students to track carefully both the range of resources taken and the language Cicero uses to describe how it was accomplished. In section 26, for example, Cicero reports that some Gauls have been forced, against their will (*invitissimi*, a term he also uses in 17), to provide military manpower, grain, money, and land. Cicero makes a similar list when citing the activities that Fonteius had to undertake as governor, and for which he now, Cicero claims, is being attacked (14). Although Cicero does not invite his audience to reflect on the consequences of such systems of extraction and greed, they were profound and I ask my students to dwell on what it might have meant for individuals and families to be subjected over generations to tactics that, as Woolf notes, had the overall effect of 'weakening and destabilizing provincial communities' (Woolf 1998, 43–4). The prominent role of private business interests in the conduct of Rome's empire, including its systems of taxation,[18] is a feature that often surprises my students, but given that some of my students are themselves business majors, this recognition can be used to generate discussion of the ways efforts to protect the investments of private corporations are often central to modern forms of extranational political domination as well. Moreover, the role of provincial economies in directing wealth to the Roman elite is underlined by the fact that the prosecutors in this case, far from being objective participants, presumably had their own financial interests in Gaul that they were seeking to protect (Dyck 2012, 13). Finally, by Cicero's accounting, the stakes of Fonteius' case could not be higher, for if the prosecution were to succeed, then provincial governors would be less likely to impose similar levies in the future, despite the necessity of such extraction for the security of the Roman state (17).

As these last two points suggest, it is important for students ultimately to consider what Cicero's speech tells us about the role of Roman legal structures in supporting the operation of Rome's empire. That law can be used to enshrine and perpetuate structures of race and inequality is not a novel idea; indeed, it is the founding principle of critical race theory, which students should be encouraged to explore when working with this speech.[19] Cicero himself is well aware of the subjective nature of law, cynically (albeit it accurately) observing that Roman law cases often involved slander and false testimony (24 and 38). So, too, Cicero openly tries to stoke the jury's ego, as well as stir their bias, by emphasizing the importance of their deliberative role (21ff), while also twice reminding them that members of the equites order in Gaul allegedly took Fonteius' side (13 and 32)—a direct appeal to class allegiance given that members of the same order were serving on the jury alongside senators. Cicero even directly invites the jury to take an active role in Rome's defense, portraying the case itself as a pseudo-war, one which the jurors must not let the Gauls win (32).

More significantly, throughout his speech, Cicero insidiously seeks to undermine the entire purpose of the *repetundae* court, which was allegedly instituted to curb abuses of power in the provinces. For by asserting that the prosecution of Fonteius is merely retribution for his conquest and subsequent authority over the Gauls (49), i.e., for the behavior routinely required of a governor from the Roman point of view, Cicero erases any meaningful distinction between imperial administration and maladministration—a stance with which, ironically, the Gauls might agree but which leaves them no avenues for reparation in law. Still, perhaps the most revealing contradiction is the fundamental paradox Cicero enthusiastically advances: namely, that people who have been structurally mistreated by Rome are, because of that experience and trauma, unfit to participate in the very legal systems ostensibly designed to redress their suffering. In this way, Cicero not only implies that the Gauls are by their nature unable to behave appropriately in a courtroom, but also that they have been made too 'bitter' by Rome's abuses to be credible witnesses to that very treatment. It is this Catch-22 that most enrages my students, who find all-too-familiar parallels in the ways law courts are designed to reward the powerful and discount the needs and voices of the most structurally vulnerable still today.

Conclusion

Woolf (1998, 28) wryly asserts that 'Rome is not the only imperial power to be better documented than its victims', and the *Pro Fonteio*, of course, prioritizes the perspective of the colonist throughout. But I have found that my students, and my Black students especially, often identify deeply with the Gauls during our discussions, and I encourage them ultimately to try to reconstruct the subjectivity of the Gauls apart from the Roman gaze presented by Cicero. Dietler (2010, 55) proposes that agency in colonial contexts 'is an active process of creative appropriation, transformation, and manipulation played out by individuals and social groups with a variety of competing interests and strategies of action embedded in local political relations and cultural perceptions.' Thus, I ask my students to read against Cicero's framing and imagine what it might have been like for people from the provinces to come to Rome and appear in a Roman court, to wear 'strange' clothing and speak a 'threatening' language. I ask them to think about why 'anger' and 'disloyalty' might be considered appropriate responses to a system that extracts so callously and so often. To consider why Indutiomarus might have spoken with defiance and not humility in the court of his enemies. Their responses to my requests are moving and often inspirational especially given that, in accordance with their own lives and experiences, many of them have little difficulty imagining such strategies of action and, indeed, routinely are in the process of devising their own.

Notes

1 Although fragmentary in its opening sections, Cicero seemingly addresses there a range of Fonteius' previous official activities, including his methods for bookkeeping while serving as urban quaestor (1–4).
2 I do not usually distinguish between imperialism and colonialism when talking about ancient Rome with my undergraduate students, although Dietler (2010, 15–16) provides a helpful overview of both terms if students want more background.
3 The designation of boundaries between groups was also fraught in the southern parts of Gaul, where ancient writers at times sought to distinguish 'Celts' or 'Gauls' from 'Ligurians' and 'Iberians'; see Dietler (2010, 79–81) and Häussler (2013, 38–47). Notably, unlike today, ancient writers did not apply the term 'Celt' to Scotland or Ireland (Dietler 1994, 585).
4 Archaeologists have traditionally used the term *oppida* or 'villages' to describe the majority of Gallic communities prior to Roman conquest (Woolf 1998, 106–12). Dietler (2010, 89), however, prefers the term '*oppidum-cités*'; for students who might be interested, Dietler's work also provides a helpful overview of Mediterranean Gaul's political structure prior to Roman conquest (88–94).
5 For a longer survey of features, begin with Isaac (2004, 424–5). Woolf (1998, 49) discusses the state of ethnographic writing prior to Roman conquest, noting the influence of Poseidonius especially on later writers.
6 In 48 C.E., emperor Claudius urged that Gauls from Gallia Comata be allowed into the Senate, an event I also discuss in my race and ethnicity course; different versions of Claudius' speech are recorded in Tacitus' *Annals* (11.23–25.1) and on the so-called Lyon tablet (*CIL* XIII, 1668) (for more on both, see Woolf 1998, 64–5).
7 In this speech, given on behalf of P. Quinctius, a Roman slave trader, Cicero notably describes Roman estates in southern Gaul, along with business activity around Narbo Martius (Woolf 1998, 42–3).
8 The dating of the speech relies, to a large extent, on the fact that Cicero says both senators and equites were serving on the jury (36) and equites had only been added to juries in 70 B.C.E. (Ward 1968, 802).
9 In terms of Cicero's continuing interest in Gaul, Woolf (1998, 29 n. 19) notes that three of his letters in 60 B.C.E. show an 'attempt to keep track of events in the interior' (*ad Att.* 1.19, 1.20, and 2.1).
10 Pompey's connections to Fonteius are suggested by passages in the *Pro Fonteio* that refer to him wintering with his troops in Transalpine Gaul and receiving financial support from Fonteius for his war efforts (12–13 and 16).
11 Smethurst collects passages from throughout Cicero's work in which he promotes Roman superiority and Rome's right to rule over others (Smethurst 1953, 219).

12 It is of limited value to ask whether Cicero 'really' held the prejudicial views he espoused in his speeches; Quintilian memorably observed that Cicero was 'flexible' when it came to the depiction of foreigners (11.1.89) and scholars have emphasized that his speeches were presumably crafted to meet the 'rhetorical exigencies of the moment,' as well as the bias of his audience (Walbank 1972, 158; cf. Vasaly 1993, 191)

13 Woolf (2011, 23) argues that the Roman fabrication of Gauls as 'ferocious, unpredictable and generally lacking in Roman virtues of discipline and dependability' allowed the Gauls to become an important 'anti-type' against which Roman identity, configured around 'stability, urbanity and rationality,' could be constructed.

14 Students might also track the word 'barbarian,' which is generally used to translate *barbarus* and holds similar connotations in both Latin and English. The tone of terms like 'tribe' or 'nation' (from *gentes* and *natio*) might be less clear in translation, but as Saddington (1961, 91–2) affirms, they were generally opposed to terms like *civitas* and *populus* in Roman thought and used of groups seen as having an inferior form of political organization.

15 Mac Sweeney (2021, 115) calls specific attention to the Greek and Roman fascination with the Gaul body and notes that the Gauls were generally credited with having lighter skin color than the Romans.

16 This was a common accusation in Roman accounts of the Gauls (Isaac 2004, 422–3); however, as Isaac points out, the Romans had themselves allegedly buried alive two Gauls and two Greeks, in accordance with the Sibylline books, in various times of crisis (422 n. 63).

17 Massilia demonstrates some of the complexity of experiences within the Roman world given both its diverse population and the fact that it could itself be perceived as a colonist in regard to the surrounding indigenous communities (Dietler 2010, 77–8).

18 Although Cicero presents all these groups as being in harmony, the attempts by Roman tax collectors *(publicani)* to extract as much profit as possible in the provinces presented a significant source of tension for Roman administrators (Steel 2001, 201). In the letter to his brother, Cicero warns that the *publicani* are especially difficult to rein in given the system's dependence on them (QFr.1.1.11–12).

19 Given its decades of development, any bibliography of key works in critical race theory would be extensive; I suggest starting with Crenshaw et al. (1995) and Delgado and Stefanic (2017).

Works Cited

Crenshaw, K., Gotanda, N., Peller, G. and Thomas, K. (eds) (1995) *Critical Race Theory: The Key Writings That Formed the Movement*, New York, NY.

Delgado, R. and Stefancic, J. (2017) *Critical Race Theory: An Introduction*, 3rd edition, New York, NY.

Dietler, M. (1994) '"Our Ancestors the Gauls": Archaeology, Ethnic Nationalism, and the Manipulation of Celtic Identity in Modern Europe', *American Anthropologist* 96.3: 584–605.

Dietler, M. (2010) *Archaeologies of Colonialism: Consumption, Entanglement, and Violence in Ancient Mediterranean France*, Berkeley, CA.

Dyck, A.R. (ed.) (2012) *Marcus Tullius Cicero: Speeches on Behalf of Marcus Fonteius and Marcus Aemilius Scaurus*, Oxford.

Fanon, F. (2004) *The Wretched of the Earth*, trans. Richard Philcox, New York, NY.

Häussler, R. (2013) 'De-Constructing Ethnic Identities: Becoming Roman in Western Cisalpine Gaul?', *BICS, Supplement* 120: 35–70.

Isaac, B. (2004) *The Invention of Racism in Classical Antiquity*, Princeton, NJ.

Mac Sweeney, N. (2021) 'Race and Ethnicity', in D.E. McCoskey (ed.), *A Cultural History of Race in Antiquity*, London, 103–18.

May, J.M. (2002) 'Cicero: His Life and Career', in J.M. May (ed.), *Brill's Companion to Cicero*, Leiden, 1–21.

Murdoch, A. (2004) 'Germania Romana', in B. Murdoch and M. Read (eds.), *Early Germanic Literature and Culture*, Rochester, NY, 55–71.

Rose, P. (1995) 'Cicero and the Rhetoric of Imperialism: Putting the Politics Back into Political Rhetoric', *Rhetorica* 13.4: 359–99.

Saddington, D.B. (1961) 'Roman Attitudes to the "Externae Gentes" of the North', *Acta Classica* 4: 90–102.

Smethurst, S.E. (1953) 'Cicero and Roman Imperial Policy', *TAPhA* 84: 216–26.

Steel, C.E.W. (2001) *Cicero, Rhetoric, and Empire*, Oxford.

Vasaly, A. (1993) *Representations: Images of the World in Ciceronian Oratory*, Berkeley, CA.

Walbank, F.W. (1972) 'Nationality as a Factor in Roman History', *HSCP* 76: 145–68.

Ward, A.M. (1968) 'Cicero's Support of Pompey in the Trials of M. Fonteius and P. Oppius', *Latomus* 27.4: 802–9.

Wells, P.S. (1995) 'Manufactured Objects and the Construction of Identities in Late La Tène Europe', *Eirene* 31: 129–50.

Williams, J.H.C. (2001) *Beyond the Rubicon: Romans and Gauls in Republican Italy*, Oxford.

Woolf, G. (1998) *Becoming Roman: The Origins of Provincial Civilization in Gaul*. Cambridge.

Woolf, G. (2011) *Tales of the Barbarians: Ethnography and Empire in the Roman West*, Malden, MA.

Wyke, M. (2007) *Caesar: A Life in Western Culture*, Chicago, IL.

5 A Classical Studies Pedagogy for the Future
An Introspective Look

Eleni Bozia

> Who controls the past controls the future. Who controls the present controls the past.
>
> George Orwell

Introduction

This chapter discusses the underpinnings of an interdisciplinary course that I developed for the Department of Classics at the University of Florida in the Fall of 2019 to move beyond traditional approaches and explore the narrative and metanarrative of the field with a focus on diversity, inclusion, and how classical studies can actualize these conversations. The course is titled "Identity of the self from classical antiquity to the digital era." It focuses on the fundamental human need to understand oneself and one's position in the world through the lens of history and its contemporaneity. Students explore how race, biological and social identities, belonging, inclusion and exclusion have been fashioned since Greco-Roman antiquity and why considerations of these civilizations are relevant to our perception of ourselves and others. This course was designed as a pedagogical experiment to prove the exigency of actionable learning and transcending conceptual disciplinary borders to better harness the lessons of Classical Studies, empower the intercultural skills the field offers, and promote its potential to contribute to the betterment of society.

Motivation

Discussions of race, ethnicity, gender identity, religion, and other descriptive attributes that make each person a unique individual, a contributing member of society, but potentially the target of

DOI: 10.4324/9781003278016-6

discriminatory behaviors as well have been at the forefront of media coverage, civic groups, political agendas, and school and university discussions in and outside of the classroom. Flawed behaviors throughout history and their perpetuation, along with more recent events, have made intolerance and social stratification even more pronounced. The lack of understanding that inevitably leads to lackluster engagement or even adversative behaviors has reached a level that needs to be urgently addressed. These topics have been and are still being dealt with in multiple different arenas. The aspect that this chapter explores deals exclusively with Classical Studies and the witting and unwitting involvement of the field in the current situation. Imperialism and slavery in the Greco-Roman societies,[1] the position of metics (foreign nationals) in ancient Athens,[2] and other negative aspects of the ancient world, including misinterpretation of the whiteness of statues[3] and the convenient "protection" of women,[4] have forced Classics scholars to come to a reckoning about what we teach our students and how.[5]

This chapter presents the methodology behind a Classics course that I developed to introduce first-year students to the Greco-Roman world through the lens of diversity. The course encourages them to study the past critically, question the *status quo* and its interpretations, and ultimately attempt a better understanding of the world around us. Discrimination, imperialism, colonization, underrepresentation, and repression of several groups, as well as the establishment of laws and practices that prolong and exacerbate such problems, have been a reality throughout the history of the world, from ancient civilizations to modern countries. Classics, ensconced in the distant past, can offer a less politicized space for people to understand the black spots of discrimination, empathize with minority groups, and reimagine a more diverse and inclusive world. To achieve these goals, Classics academics need to contemporize their courses, infusing them with a degree of realism and practicality.[6]

Narrative and Meta-Narrative of Greco-Roman Antiquity in an Interconnected World

The study of Greco-Roman antiquity has been considered irrelevant, impractical, and elitist. As a result, Classicists find themselves in the unenviable position of explaining the purpose of their work to students, the public, and the university administration. At the same time, Classics graduates may not always seem or feel competitive in the job market. And in pre-university education, ancient Greek and Latin are only offered in select schools.[7] Additionally, Classics has been misused throughout history by misguided agendas,[8] but this can be said about other disciplines too. Conversely, few people question the value of history and its lessons. The histories of modern nations have proven that accepting your past and embracing improvement and change is possible. So, how can we come to terms with the history of our field, embrace its challenges, and come out with a stronger discipline that contributes to the social good? In his acceptance speech for the Nobel Prize for Literature, Kazuo Ishiguro contemplated these issues on a much larger scale: 'At Birkenau, on a wet afternoon, I stood before the rubbled remains of the gas chambers - now strangely neglected and unattended...Should these remains be protected?...Or should they be allowed, slowly and naturally, to rot away to nothing?...Are there times when forgetting is the only way to stop cycles of violence, or to stop a society disintegrating into chaos and war? On the other hand, can stable, free nations really build on foundations of willful amnesia and frustrated justice?'[9]

The two actionable ways to actively engage Classics in these conversations are to show the discipline's relevance for all people beyond the cisgender, white, male, western bubble and teach the students to move beyond the obvious. To this end, I make sure to present and discuss research of the Greco-Roman world not as the center of world heritage but as one piece in the puzzle of world heritage with a view to considering what the study of the classical past can contribute to our understanding of the self, society, and the world. For example, when you walk into a museum, the collections may be thematic—the prehistoric world with its Sumerian, Hittite, Minoan, and Mycenaean components, later the Egyptian, Greek, and Roman worlds, and so on. One will reasonably think it is historically accurate to present the exhibits in this configuration. However, in other cases, we see entire floors that showcase the history of the ancient Greek world and then a whole other floor dedicated to the Roman and another to the Near East. One might see the reasoning behind both. But the first worldview approach is more likely to instill a sense of world cultural heritage in the public and assign credit to other civilizations for some of the inspiration for artistic and cerebral exchanges with the Greek and Roman world. It may also very well suggest a different way to study Classics and make it relevant outside of the western world.[10]

With a view to re-examining otherness, the ancient Greek novels are a treasure trove of such articulations as they present others through the eyes of the Greeks. So, as the scope of class readings is to change the focus and perspective, I ask the students to study the Greeks and

Romans through the eyes of others. Reid (1996) discusses the history of Classics as a discipline and a field of inquiry in Egypt within the latter's context. From Afro-Caribbean and African American receptions of Classics and hip-hop brushes with Greek history[11] to immigrant communities who can see themselves in the face of Aeneas,[12] criticize Juvenal's castigation of Greeks, Jews, and other Easterners as polluting Rome,[13] or empathize with Cicero's proclamation that "denying foreigners access to the city is truly inhumane" (*Off.* 3.47),[14] Classics should be about all people and for all people. Therefore, such comparative readings and analyses enhance students' appreciation of otherness through historical perspectives and modern comparanda.

Course Syllabus

The course that I developed is geared explicitly toward first-year undergraduate students, focuses on an interdisciplinary narrative, and critically explores the past through the eyes of the present and vice versa. During the first half of the semester, the students read selections of ancient Greek and Latin literature as well as secondary bibliography to get a comprehensive understanding of the topics of gender, immigration, bilingualism/translingualism, and identity and belonging from literary sources, laws, and inscriptions as well as current discussions on related current events. During the second half, they learn about and use digital tools to enhance their voice, consider the significance of digital preservation, and ultimately reappreciate their footprint in the world as this will be the future generations' past.

We begin the semester by expanding our worldview and rethinking all the established definitions of race, ethnicity, ethnic identity, and other popular classifications. And we make sure to ask the right questions: Why is a whole group of people named after the Caucasus Mountain range? And why did Blumenbach, the father of what was initially a scientific classification expressed in anthropological terms, when filtered through politics, become the rallying cry of Nazism against the backdrop of a wrongly assumed unadulterated Greek purity?[15] Next, my students are assigned chapters from *Sapiens: A Brief History of Humankind* as a way to broaden their perspective regarding our origins as a species.[16] They are then asked to read Hippocrates' *Air, Water, and Places* to explore bioclimatology and its effects on human health and appearance. Additional scientific readings on the relationship or lack thereof between our environment and our DNA prompt the students to combine methodological and interdisciplinary approaches to understand any given topic and reconsider long-established views on how we see people (both literally and figuratively) and how science can masquerade as pseudo-science.

Next, we turn our attention to the ancient Greeks, their claims to autochthony, pride in democracy, and their reception throughout history. The reading assignments include Aeschylus' *Persians* against the backdrop of Peter Brook's *Orghast* and Mozart's *Die Entführung aus dem Serail* (The abduction from the Seraglio).[17] Democratic institutions and the right to citizenship and equity are fundamental human rights. However, due to systemic legal gaps, complacency due to the inertia of existing if not consistently enforced laws, and a slew of other socio-political reasons, they are not enjoyed by all. Aristotle's *Politics*, Euripides' *Ion*, and Demosthenes 57 *Against Eubulides* frame our class discussion to consider current immigration and tax laws and treaties in the US, Europe, and any other country that the students choose to study. We then read Euripides' *Medea* and Alice Walker's *The Color Purple* to explore socially disenfranchised foreign women and women of color.[18]

Subsequently, the course continues with a close study of the Roman Empire. Through primary and secondary readings, the students are invited to explore the expansion of a small city in Latium with its particularities in how it developed, according to both Livy and Dionysius Halicarnassus, into a multilingual and multicultural empire. Imperialism, colonialism, slavery, and the idea of freedom are all concepts on which students reflect, while I also prompt them to go behind the sources and consider the authorship of those narratives and the significance of literary representation for all. To this end, we read passages from the elite *literati* alongside chapters from Edward Said's *Culture and Imperialism* and Chinua Achebe's *Home and Exile*. Conversely, we study Claudius' Lyon Tablet and his entreaty to the Roman Senate to admit Gauls as members, Caracalla's *Constitutio Antoniana*, and several selections from Lucian and Apuleius—nonnative speakers of Greek and Latin, respectively—and other translingual authors. Consequently, students learn what it meant to be a citizen with rights and responsibilities. Students learn well as about the stratifications, discriminations, and inclusivity or lack thereof in the Greco-Roman world.

Circling back to the employability of a Classics graduate, the course also focuses on the skills that a student can get. So, from a professor's perspective, the central question is: How can we turn the study of Classics into actionable learning, learning for living? Consider when you were a child and read fairy tales. It is not so much about Little Red Riding Hood and the wolf but more about danger and being alert when approached by a stranger. Stories, history, and histories teach us facts and the morals behind the facts. They can also teach us how to think, parse these stories and events, and use them wisely without having to make the same mistakes.

So, it is not only about Pericles' citizenship law that required both parents to be Athenian citizens for a child to have citizenship, but it is also about any modern society that grapples with issues of inclusion, any child who was born to undocumented parents, and anyone who has been asked: "No, where are you really from?"[19] What can a student who wishes to study tax law possibly learn from *Inscriptiones Graecae*? Perhaps that the first classifications between permanent residents and business travelers regarding taxation were put forward in ancient Athens (*IG* II 2 141.30–36). What can one possibly learn from Demosthenes 57 when Euxitheus has to defend his birthright? Perhaps an early lesson into modern politics and the infamous birther movement.[20] Regarding citizenship and representation, what is a better place to start than inclusion and exclusion in ancient Athens that echoed in the nineteenth- and twentieth-century U.S.? Women's rights have been at the forefront in the past several years. And 'women's rights' typically refers to the progress made since the suffrage movement in the nineteenth century. What about Penelope[21] and Medea,[22] then? Finally, everyone is appalled at war crimes, but how many of us have done something about an event when it feels too far away? Perhaps it would help if younger generations, who will be the lawmakers, the NGO volunteers, the military attachés, and soldiers on duty, realized the millennia-old horrors brought to the fore by Thucydides' narrative of Melos' treatment by the Athenians.

On the other hand, the Roman Empire has something else to teach us, namely the extension of immigration laws, the naturalization of everyone, and an Empire that is bi- and multilingual. Of course, it also makes it timely to talk about colonialism and the eradication of local dialects under Roman rule, a discussion that leads to modern colonization and the fate of African languages.[23] But we should also acknowledge Roman open-mindedness and ancient Greek multicultural and multidialectal existence that occasionally is less accepted in our world. Social justice, equity, and representation in the high echelons of each government have been goals that we have yet to reach. Yet Septimius Severus was an African Emperor whose artistic representation was not whitewashed for the sake of purity. How many modern countries can say the same?

Politics of life are not just an issue of politicians. Each of us has a personal life and a societal one. Regardless of our path in life, whether we get a job in the public or private sector or become stay-at-home parents, we experience the world around us, have certain expectations for us and others, and our choices have an effect on everyone. Overall, the course frames such discussions and considerations in a constant back-and-forth between the past and the present that advances our understanding of the Greco-Roman world but can also illuminate the present.

Digitizing the Past, Connecting with the Present, Preparing for the Future

The second part of the course examines the importance of understanding and appreciating histories and cultures through technology. More specifically, it explores how digital technologies and digital preservation can help us build connections between different histories and cultures and create a space where we value our local and national pasts while recognizing and appreciating our connection to those of others. Assignments include the development of a digital story followed by 3D scanning and 3D printing sessions to actualize a tangible relationship with the world's past(s) and better comprehend our connections through concepts, objects, and sites.[24]

More specifically, students are assigned to develop a digital story to actualize issues of exclusion. In addition, they have to create a video in class, using any free software to vocalize and share their understanding of Athenian citizenship, inclusion, or lack thereof and relate it to personal thoughts and experiences. Some students write the script, another group performs the skit, and others oversee the video production. Overall, students are in charge of authoring their narrative and becoming aware that technology can help amplify their voice but may also create a noise that requires that one is constantly and critically aware.[25]

Furthermore, during visits to the Harn Museum of Art and the Florida Museum of Natural History, we 3D digitize artifacts from Greco-Roman antiquity, Africa, Asia, or Indigenous peoples.[26] Students then visit the Marston Science Library at the University of Florida to 3D print the models and write a reflection piece on their appreciation of world heritage, the significance of all histories and cultures, and the problems with museum colonization that can be exacerbated by digital technologies if, left unregulated.[27] Concurrently, in our class meetings, we discuss digitization and world heritage as students reflect on the impact of technology on our lives and contextualize our history with that of our peers worldwide. Additionally, on a strictly academic level, they come to appreciate how interdisciplinary studies can deepen our understanding of any research object.

Such a conscious approach to world heritage aims to foster the realization that ancient remains, historical sites, documents, tablets, inscriptions, books, pamphlets, and recordings are what previous generations have left us. By closely studying all those objects throughout the course and then moving to our digital present, students better comprehend that their present will be future generations' past.[28] Likewise, their social media postings and the other technologies they will develop in their careers and use throughout their lives will inevitably be their footprint. So, the ways we appreciate differences, promote connections with our communities and the world, and showcase all that in our everyday life and encounters are our cultural footprint.[29]

Conclusion

In closing, Marc Twain is quoted as saying, "History doesn't repeat itself, but it often rhymes." We can all appreciate the teachings of history and the collective wisdom of centuries and civilizations past that can shed light on our understanding of the world. However, how can we be active agents in this process and translate this into an actualized way of living? Can Classics, a discipline firmly grounded in the study of the past, be the conduit between the past, the present, and the future? Beyond the history and the morals, the beauty of the texts, and the unique experience of reconstructing an era that existed so long ago, the pedagogical approaches that I have developed bring students to an advantageous position to critically approach situations and crises that have already developed and been dealt with, examine their impact, propose other solutions, and experiment safely. The modern readings also enable them to see themselves as parts of world history and active members of multiple societies on a national and international level. Looking into the past intentionally and critically can make everyone a conscious and self-actualized citizen. The Linear B tablets from Pylos give us a fleeting insight into everyday Mycenaean life. What are our "Pylos tablets?" What will our cultural mark be? Such questions, explorations, and reflections can make Classics courses a space for catalytic social improvement.

Notes

1 For an acerbic and realistic apprehension of the state of affairs in the teaching of Classics, see Robinson (2017).
2 Euripides' *Ion* offers an insight into metics. For a study of *Ion* and its implications for issues of autochthony and citizenship, see Kasimis' (2018) profound consideration of the play against the backdrop of metic status 42–8 and Lape (2010, 95–136). For general discussions of the topics,

consult the contributions in Boegehold and Scafuro (1994) and their respective bibliographical references. See also Kennedy's (2014) analysis of the status of metic women.
3 A critical publication on the issue is Bond (2017).
4 For modern discussions of the position of women in the ancient world and modern contextualization, see Eilberg-Schwartz and Doniger (1995); van Zyl Smit (2002); Beard (2017).
5 For discussion, see Bostick (2020).
6 There are a lot of resources on best practices for diversifying Classics and cultivating more community engagements. Some representative examples include Murray (2019); Rankine (2019); Steward and Machado (2019).
7 Hall (2015). These dynamics also explain the multitude of online publications and discussions around the topic of why one should study Classics.
8 For discussions, see Dee (2003–2004); Allen (2015). See Zuckerberg (2018) for an extensive relevant bibliography. See also Pharos (https://pharos.vassarspaces.net/) that offers suggestions as on how one should navigate efficiently and avoid misappropriations of classical antiquity.
9 Ishiguro (2017, 22–3; 25).
10 See van Weyenberg (2013) and Malamud (2016) for discussions of the role of Classics in societies and cultures beyond the western world.
11 Padilla Peralta (2015a).
12 See O'Neill and Rigoni (2021) for modern readings of the *Aeneid* and the latter's intersection with contemporary immigration narratives.
13 See Moodie (2014) for a close reading of *Satire 3* and Juvenal's representation of the city and its corruption that is blamed on "the others." On foreigners and prejudice in Juvenal, see Gallia (2016); Moore (1976); Watts (1976); Gellérfi (2019).
14 Padilla Peralta (2015b).
15 For a detailed presentation, consult Diamond (1994).
16 Harari (2018)
17 Hall (2007) offers an incisive contrapuntal analysis of Aeschylus' play and its modern adaptations.
18 See Cutter (2000) for a discussion of the work and Parker (2010) for a discussion of the feminine and the role of embroidery.
19 See https://www.cnn.com/interactive/2017/08/opinion/where-im-really-from/
20 See https://dictionary.cambridge.org/us/dictionary/english/birther
21 See Clark (2001).
22 See van Zyl Smit (2002).
23 See Adams et al. (2002); Adams (2003) for an in-depth study of bilingualism. Cf. wa Thiong'o N. (1986, 5–13, 19–20) (*et passim*) who emphasizes the significance of writing in African languages instead of English as a means of preserving the culture and establishing one's own voice and narrative.
24 See Di Giuseppantonio di Franco et al. (2018); Bozia (2023) for the significance of digitization and accessibility of world heritage sites and artifacts.
25 This is an example of an individual story that was developed: https://vimeo.com/356253835
26 Vincent, J. (2020) 'How a designer used AI and Photoshop to bring ancient Roman emperors back to life' https://www.theverge.com/2020/8/21/21395115/roman-emperors-photorealistic-portraits-ai-artbreeder-dan-voshart

27 Pavis, M. and Wallace, A. (2019) offer an informative and hard-to-ignore report on intellectual property rights.
28 For a relevant discussion, see Danto (2008) and Jacks (2008).
29 On cultural footprint, see Baltà Portolés and Roig Madorran (2011).

Works Cited

Adams, J. (2003) Bilingualism and the Latin Language, Cambridge.
Adams, J., Janse, M. and Swain, S. (2002) *Bilingualism in Ancient Society*, Oxford.
Allen, C. (2015) 'Ovid's *Metamorphoses* Now Deemed Too "Triggering" for Students at Columbia', *Independent Women's Forum*, 13 May.
Baltà Portolés, J. and Roig Madorran, E. (2011) *Approaches to Cultural Footprint*, Brussels.
Beard, M. (2017) *Women & Power*, London.
Boegehold, A.L. and Scafuro, A.C. (eds.) (1994) *Athenian Identity and Civic Ideology*, Baltimore, MD.
Bond, S. (2017) 'Whitewashing Ancient Statues: Whiteness, Racism And Color In The Ancient World', *Forbes*, 27 April.
Bostick, D. (2020) 'Not for All: Nostalgic Distortions as a Weapon of Segregation in Secondary Classics', *American Journal of Philology* 141.2: 283–306.
Bozia, E. (2023) '"Please, Touch the Exhibit": 3D Archaeology for Experiential Spatialization,' in G. Landeschi and E. Betts (eds.) *Capturing the Senses*, Cham.
Chinua, A. (2001) *Home and Exile*, London.
Clark, M. (2001) 'Was Telemachus Rude to His Mother? *Odyssey* 1.356–9', *Classic Philology* 96.4: 335–54.
Cutter, M.J. (2000) 'Philomela Speaks: Alice Walker's Revisioning of Rape Archetypes in The Color Purple', *MELUS* 25.3–4: 161–80.
Danto, A.C. (2008) 'The Past in the Present', *Places* 20.1: 30–1.
Dee, J. (2003–2004) 'Black Odysseus, White Caesar: When Did "White People" Become "White"? *The Classical Journal* 99: 157–67.
Diamond, J. (1994) 'Race Without Color', Discover Magazine, 1 November.
Di Giuseppantonio Di Franco, P., Galeazzi, F., and Vassallo, V. (eds.) (2018) *Authenticity and Cultural Heritage in the Age of 3D Digital Reproductions*, Cambridge.
Eilberg-Schwartz, H. and Doniger, W. (eds.) (1995) *Off with Her Head! The Denial of Women's Identity in Myth, Religion, and Culture*, Berkeley, CA.
Gallia, A. (2016) '"Some of My Best Friends..." Reading Prejudice in Juvenal's Third Satire', *The Classical Journal* 111.3: 319–46.
Gellérfi, G. (2019) 'Xenophobic Utterances in Juvenal's Satires', *Graeco-Latina Brunensia* 24.1: 81–91.
Hall, E. (2007) 'Aeschylus' Persians via the Ottoman Empire to Saddam Hussein', in E. Bridges, E. Hall and P.J. Rhodes (eds.), *Cultural Responses to the Persian Wars*, Oxford, 167–200.

Hall, E. (2015) 'Classics for the People—Why We Should All Learn from the Ancient Greeks', *The Guardian*, 20 June.
Harari, Y.N. (2018) *Sapiens. A Brief History of Humankind*, London.
Ishiguro, K. (2017) *My Twentieth Century Evening and Other Small Breakthroughs. The Nobel Lecture*, London.
Jacks, P. (2008) 'Restauratio and Reuse: The Afterlife of Roman Ruins', *Places* 20.1: 10–20.
Kasimis, D. (2018) *The Perpetual Immigrant and the Limits of Athenian Democracy*, Cambridge.
Kennedy, R.F. (2014) *Immigrant Women in Athens*, London.
Lape, S. (2010) *Race and Citizen Identity in the Classical Athenian Democracy*, Cambridge.
Malamud, M. (2016) *African Americans and the Classics*, London.
Moodie, E. (2014) 'Umbricius' Farewell Tour', *The Classical World* 108.1: 27–44.
Moore, P. (1976) 'Juvenal and the Orontes', *The Classical World* 69.6: 376–7.
Murray, J. (2019) 'W.E.B. Du Bois' The Quest of the Silver Fleece: The Education of Black Medea', *TAPhA* 149.2: 143–62.
O'Neill, J.R. and Rigoni, A. (2021) *The Aeneid and the Modern World*, London.
Padilla Peralta, D. (2015a) 'From Damocles to Socrates', *Eidolon*, 8 June.
Padilla Peralta, D. (2015b) 'Barbarians Inside the Gate, Part 1', *Eidolon*, 5 November.
Parker, R. (2010) *The Subversive Stitch: Embroidery and the Making of the Feminine*, London.
Pavis, M. and Wallace, A. (2019) 'Response to the 2018 Sarr-Savoy Report: Statement on Intellectual Property Rights and Open Access Relevant to the Digitization and Restitution of African Cultural Heritage and Associated Materials', *Journal of Intellectual Property, Information Technology and E-Commerce Law* 10.2: 115–29.
Rankine, P.D. (2019) 'The Classics, Race, and Community-Engaged or Public Scholarship', *American Journal of Philology* 140.2: 345–59.
Reid, D.M. (1996) 'Cromer and the Classics: Imperialism, Nationalism and the Greco-Roman Past in Modern Egypt', *Middle Eastern Studies* 32.1: 1–29.
Robinson, E. (2017) '"The Slaves Were Happy": High School Latin and the Horrors of Classical Studies', *Eidolon*, 25 September.
Said, E. (1994) *Culture and Imperialism*, London.
Steward, S. and Machado, D. (2019) 'Progress and Precarity: 150 Years of TAPA', *TAPhA* 149.2: 39–60.
van Weyenberg, A. (2013) *The Politics of Adaptation*, Amsterdam.
van Zyl Smit, B. (2002) 'Medea the Feminist', *Acta Classica* 45: 101–22.
Watts, W.J. (1976) 'Race Prejudice in the Satires of Juvenal', *Acta Classica* 19: 83–104.
wa Thiong'o, N. (1986) *Decolonizing the Mind*, Portsmouth, NH.
Zuckerberg, D. (2018) *Not All Dead White Men*, Cambridge, MA.

6 Looking Up, Looking Online

Gender, Representation, and Bias in Classics*

Victoria Leonard

In 1908, Edith Morley became the first woman in the history of Higher Education in the UK to be appointed as a Professor.[1] Rather than a glorious culmination and recognition of the achievements of women, Morley had to force the appointment at University College, Reading, now the University of Reading, after she was the only member of the otherwise all-male department not promoted. Her insistence on the promotion a year later than the rest of her department had rebarbative consequences: Morley was made a Professor of English Language rather than her specialism of English Literature, and her Chair would be abolished on her retirement, negating her legacy, as she felt it.[2] Morley was subject to considerable gender discrimination and stigmatisation throughout her career, surviving rather than flourishing in an adverse environment.

Morley's appointment was a significant benchmark for the history of women in Higher Education, setting a precedent for the place of women within the professoriate. Yet it would take a staggering 111 years before the first black woman would reach the same professional level in the field of Classics. A year after the Royal Historical Society's *Race, Ethnicity and Equality Report* found that only 0.5% of historians working in UK universities were black, Katherine Harloe was appointed Professor of Classics at Morley's former workplace, the University of Reading, becoming the first black Professor of Classics in the UK in 2019.[3]

The lack of diversity in Classics is, unhappily, not exceptional across the Humanities. A black woman was appointed to the professoriate in the field of History only in 2018, with Olivette Otele's promotion to Professor at Bath Spa University.[4] Whilst Otele expressed optimism on her appointment, hoping that it would 'open the door for many hard-working women, especially black women in academia,' she also recognised the cost of success: 'It's hard. I'm tired. It's bleak.'[5]

DOI: 10.4324/9781003278016-7

Like Morley, Otele's appointment met with opposition; as Sadiah Qureshi has pointed out, a black woman making history during October's Black History Month was perceived as a conspiracy. It was, in fact, a coincidence—the University of Bath Spa announce all results of applications for professorships in October following their submission in the spring.[6]

The calculated apathy and snail-pace progress of these appointments are not coincidences or anomalies. They are the very tip of the iceberg of systemic marginalisation and intersectional bias that coalesces into a toxic mix of racism, sexism, classism, and ableism that holds back women and non-binary people, disabled people, those from lower socio-economic backgrounds, and those from minority ethnic backgrounds. This chapter aims not only to outline disadvantage, marginalisation, and injustice in Classics, but to show how bias and discrimination are determined by larger structural and systemic factors. Whilst discrimination often presents as an isolated incident or as a series of unrelated anomalies or coincidences, it does, in fact, function as a pattern.

When we look up, who do we see? The systemic nature of discrimination that constrains models of success is evident if we focus our attention laterally across highly visible contexts such as learned societies and decision-making institutions like governments. Statues of men grossly outnumber statues of women in the UK, with only 2.7% of civic statues featuring historical, non-royal women.[7] Only 14% of blue plaques celebrate women,[8] and only 2% commemorate black people.[9] Positions of authority are dominated by men: 66% of MPs sitting in the House of Commons are men, and 72% of Peers in the House of Lords are men.[10] Just 10% of the Royal Society are female, and in over 300 years, there has only been one woman Speaker of the House of Commons.[11] When we look up, we see a monolithic type of success that is impossible to replicate beyond a narrow typology.

In higher education contexts, although women dominate at postgraduate levels, the proportion of women declines at every stage of the academic career path, beginning with the postdoctoral and early-career phase. By the professoriate, only 28% of professors in UK universities are women.[12] At the current rate of change, the professoriate will not be representative in terms of gender balance until 2043. Less than 1% of professors in the UK are black, at only 155 out of more than 23,000 professors.[13] Less than a third of top universities were led by women (9 out of 29) in 2021.[14] The number of black academics in the most senior positions in UK universities is officially zero, as HESA's latest data collection from 2018 to 2019 shows.[15] Only 1.2% of UKRI

Research Council studentships were awarded to Black of Black Mixed students (245 out of 19,868).[16] Less than 1% of UKRI Fellows were from the black ethnic group, and less than 1% of Principal Investigators (PIs) were black, according to data published in 2020.[17] Women in higher education are disproportionately burdened with administrative and pastoral roles whilst they are over-represented in precarious and part-time positions.[18] In addition, women are subject to a significant gender pay gap, earning 14.7% less than male colleagues, a disparity that is higher in the wider labour market.[19] These statistics reveal what Patricia Hill Collins terms the 'matrix of domination' in action, which is characterised by intersecting oppressions.[20]

Similar levels of discrimination and imbalance are evident if we turn to the field of Classics, looking specifically at gendered recognition by learned societies, national academies, and gender biases within publishing. Within the British Academy's Fellowship scheme for Classical Antiquity, only 10% of Corresponding Fellows and 20% of Ordinary Fellows are women. The Classical Association, the Society for the Promotion of Hellenic Studies, and the Society for the Promotion of Roman Studies have been electing presidents for more than a century, and yet the proportion of women presidents remains between 8% and 13%.[21]

Corresponding levels of underrepresentation are evident in high-prestige journals such as the *Journal of Roman Studies*, where 22% of published articles 2005–2019 were authored by women.[22] Seventy-six percent of submissions received by the Journal *Classical Quarterly* 2010–2019 were authored by men. Twenty-four percent of articles published by the Journal of Hellenic Studies, 2005–2018, were written by women. Men authored 71% of all articles submitted for consideration, and there was 8% gender gap between acceptance (24% for men and 14% for women).[23] Accessing higher levels of seniority, pay grades, prestige, and recognition within Classics is subject to gendered constraints; for men, the chances of success are higher, the process is quicker, and the historical dominance of men means that there are always comfortable models available to follow.

These statistics tell us two important things. First, it shows us that these problems are all related: the struggle to break into or break apart a paradigm that enables a very narrow type of success in order for women, non-binary people, and those from minority ethnic backgrounds to access the most senior decision-making roles in higher education is part of a wider pattern across society. Classics does not have a unique problem.[24] This type of pattern recognition invalidates arguments that the dominance of a certain type of person at senior levels of employment is meritocratic or a coincidence, or that women are not interested in these roles, or that they are biologically more suited to caring or service roles that are, again not coincidentally, less valued and remunerated on a much lower scale. Discerning the pattern of discrimination counteracts scarcity bias, or the position that optimum levels of equality have been achieved where a person of colour, a non-binary person, or a woman has succeeded, and that further representation would be a dangerous overrepresentation.[25]

Second, these statistics demonstrate that we are not finished with foremothers and firsts, that the need to notice the kind of exceptional bench-marking progress and the unprecedented achievements of women or people from marginalised or disadvantaged backgrounds are not the strict preserve of the nineteenth century. Despite the beguiling language of inclusivity and diversity marketed by companies, platforms, and institutions, significant obstacles to inclusion and diversity remain at all levels of society. Women, non-binary people and people of colour are looked at, but they are still not seen. We need our trailblazers now more than ever.[26]

Thirty-five years ago, Gerda Lerner outlined the androcentric fallacy, where the subordination of women by men was premised on their internalised inferiority, enabling women to accept the myth that they had no history.[27] Lerner foregrounded the distortion of the historical record that legitimised the male version of history as normative and accepted as a universal truth.[28] But this distortion is not limited to the past. The assumption that sexism is part of history and therefore would not be found in new technologies such as the internet is erroneous, and online environments have evolved to maintain the marginalisation of women and non-binary people.[29] Archives, including those online, are not neutral, and the labour of noticing, recording, and celebrating firsts and foremothers is not automatic, and it is not unproblematic. This is particularly evident on Wikipedia.

The world's largest and most open-access repository of knowledge, Wikipedia, has significant biases, particularly against women and non-binary people, as represented subjects with biographical pages, and as contributing editors.[30] Wikipedia is arguably *the* interface between humans and knowledge. The online encyclopaedia contains more than six million articles, with an average of nearly 600 new articles added every day. Its user rates are phenomenal, with 21 billion page views in November 2021 alone.[31] It is the thirteenth most visited website in the world, attracting more traffic than Zoom, Twitter, and Instagram.[32] If you use the internet, you use Wikipedia. Text-based search engines like Google and voice-enabled search applications like Siri and Alexa scrape Wikipedia for information. With Google's Instant Answers, the user consumes information derived from Wikipedia without even clicking on a link.[33] Particularly as a first rather than a final resource, the answer to the question, how do we know things, is often Wikipedia.

What are the consequences when a platform as significant as Wikipedia in determining our cognitive intake marginalises non-binary people and women, especially women of colour, and elides their achievements? Between 84% and 91% of editors are men, a dominance of the male perspective that produces unbalanced content, with only 19% of biographies on English-language Wikipedia featuring women.[34] That skew is even more apparent when it comes to Classics: an estimate in 2016 found that only 7% of biographies of classicists featured women.[35] This meant that while no particular effort was needed for male classicists to be well represented with detailed Wikipedia pages, before focused campaigns such as #WCCWiki, trailblazing classicists such as Dorothy Tarrant, the first woman Professor of Greek in the UK, and the first woman president of the Classical Association, was notably absent from Wikipedia, despite her evident notability.

The implications of this online bias are wide-ranging. As an encyclopaedia, Wikipedia is a tertiary source, meaning that it gathers together existing information in one place, rather than presenting original research. The absence of women and non-binary classicists on Wikipedia reflects a wider absence of available information about them online, but it also re-inscribes existing absences from other cultures of knowledge whilst pretending to compile and collect 'everything.'

The online encyclopaedia is also the closest we have come to truly open-access knowledge, and it has the potential to transform how easily accessible information is, with a biographical page flowing readily into other sources of information to be reworked by journalists, editors, publishers, and institutions. This higher level of visibility can have a significant impact on the opportunities women can access, their chances of promotion, and how their legacy is preserved and celebrated. As Lucy Moore and Richard Nevell have argued, amplification works both ways; centring whiteness and excluding people of colour and their histories on Wikipedia disseminates on a global scale, perpetuating the racial and gender biases of editors.[36]

Online gender bias is both product and cause of the same outcome: whilst the contributions of women are siloed into obscurity, the field is skewed towards male and white dominance. This archive, through its

Looking Up, Looking Online 77

elision of women's achievements in the academy and elsewhere, represents a world in which almost only men are capable of excellence. In this way, the patriarchal sub-structure of the archive and the academy are made to appear ordinary, natural and factual, even biological, rather than ideological.

The elision of women and non-binary people is not only an injustice to those individuals. Discarding their achievements contributes to the institutional violence that excludes them from academic positions, discounting them from the imagined future of knowledge production when promotions and appointments are decided. When we look up, instead of seeing women and non-binary people and their achievements, we are presented with a distorted illustration of knowledge that paints them only as accessories, aides, or absurd pretenders.

How do women fix their past and future at the same time as operating in the present? One answer, which is also part of the problem, is Wikipedia. To challenge the gendered absence of classicists (broadly conceived) who identify as women and non-binary on Wikipedia, the Women's Classical Committee UK (WCC) organised the initiative #WCCWiki in 2017.[37] The WCC UK was founded in 2015 to promote feminist and gender-informed perspectives on ancient Mediterranean cultures, paralleling the US-based Women's Classical Caucus that was founded in 1972.[38] Before the WCC's foundation, there was no gender-orientated Classics organisation in the UK. The first #WCCWiki editing event alone doubled the representation of women classicists on Wikipedia. #WCCWiki brings people of all genders together, pre-pandemic at least, in-person at training sessions and conferences, and through monthly online sessions, to create and improve pages for archaeologists, historians, classicists, theologians, art historians, theorists, and philosophers. Indeed, the initiative has received pushback, not for crossing the boundaries between disciplines or international borders, but for not making pages for men. The community response of online activism to discrimination has transformed the heritage of women in Classics, both historical and contemporary, from a largely unrepresented online demographic to a highly visible and accessible part of the field.[39]

#WCCWiki makes it possible to look up women when looking online. The #WCCWiki community has created or edited more than 600 Wikipedia pages for women, including those women whose achievements were forgotten and who were only referred to on their husband's pages, such as Dr Miriam T. Griffin, Dr Annie Ure, Professor Gillian Clark, and Professor Leslie Brubaker.[40] #WCCWiki's pace of change means that on average every other day, a women's page is created or edited. #WCCWiki articles have featured regularly on Wikipedia's front page, and #WCCWiki has inspired international franchises, from Durham in the UK, to Winnipeg in Canada, to Ohio in the US.[41] Hundreds of thousands of people have viewed #WCCWiki pages, with their impact boosted on social media, where posts have reached 50,000+ people. #WCCWiki articles have received the Good Article classification on Wikipedia, and the initiative has been integrated into undergraduate and postgraduate teaching in Classics at universities in the UK.[42]

In July 2021, Wikipedia featured 454 biographical pages of women classicists, which is 17.7% of the total.[43] #WCCWiki's incremental progress is demonstrated by Richard Nevell's analysis, which found that 384 pages for women classicists constituted 16.3% of the total in December 2019, and 268 pages for women classicists constituted 12.8% of the total in December 2018.[44] The number of new biographical pages on classicists in 2019 was 271, and the scale of #WCCWiki's contribution is demonstrated by the proportion that featured women: 42.8%, a dramatic reversal from previous years. By comparison, in the same year, only 13% and 14% of new biographies written about classicists in German and French were about women, highlighting how extreme the male bias can skew online representation without collective action.[45]

But despite the huge effort of #WCCWiki, the scale of the problem means that the overall percentage of pages for classicists that feature women is still only around 20%, which is consistent with Wikipedia's wider gender bias where pages for women are outnumbered 5:1 by pages for men. The WCC Wikidata Redlist records 1,800 women classicists that still do not have pages, with the WCC's crowd-sourced list of missing pages adds a further 109 to the total, and those are only the ones that have been noticed and recorded.[46] Women who have made significant contributions to the field still lack proper representation online.

Challenging gendered bias may seem straightforward: create more pages for notable women and non-binary classicists. But a rising tide does not raise all boats, and representation alone does not eradicate discrimination. Sexism, racism, and misogyny make increasing representation more difficult than it should be. Pages for women are targeted with vandalism, disruptive editing, and abuse, creating an adverse environment for women editors and for editors working to improve the representation of women and non-binary people online. Women are 27 times more likely to face abuse online than men, and black women in particular receive the most abuse from strangers on social media.[47] We can see how online violence silences women in the stark gender imbalance of

Wikipedia editors: around 9/10 are men.[48] Consequently, fewer pages for women and non-binary people are created, stages of review can stymie attempted page creations, and those that are created have more difficulty 'sticking': pages for women are more likely to get tagged as problematic, considered not notable, or deleted.[49]

Undoing or 'reverting' more spectacular forms of vandalism and abuse directed towards particularly visible Wikipedia pages can be achieved quickly and easily. As the author of a book about the appropriation of Classics by online misogynist groups, it is hardly surprising that the page for Donna Zuckerburg would attract the attention of anonymous editors using violent, insulting, and anti-Semitic language.[50] Priyamvada Gopal's page has been used to attack her on political and racial grounds, and Mary Beard's page has been persistently targeted with disruptive editing, deriding her appearance and age.[51] The pages for historical women can similarly be subject to abuse and vandalism, as shown by Wikipedia's page for the Ivory Bangle Lady, a Christian woman who was originally from north Africa and who was buried in York in the fourth century CE.[52] These types of edits are easy to revert, and targeted pages can be given protected status by administrators. But micro-aggressions and unconscious bias rooted in misogyny and racism are harder to detect and as a result, more difficult to challenge and revert.

Challenges to notability are a particularly effective way to undermine the status of women on Wikipedia without resorting to abuse or vandalism. Wikipedia has guidelines rather than rules that a subject has to be notable before having a Wikipedia page, and academics should fulfil at least one of eight criteria to be considered notable, most commonly being a Professor or holding a named Chair.[53] But the guidelines for notability are not applied uniformly and, as in the rest of society, women and people of colour are held to much higher standards.

The biased application of notability drew attention in 2018 following the award of a Nobel Prize to Donna Strickland, only the third woman to receive the award in Physics.[54] An attempt to create a page featuring Strickland's already high-level achievements was denied in 2014, with the subject not considered notable enough and the page was deleted in less than six minutes.[55] Editors have since worked hard to keep this aspect of Strickland's biography off the page itself, endlessly picking over the now irrelevant issue of her notability.[56] Clarice Phelps, a black nuclear scientist who helped to discover the chemical element, Tennessine, and the first African-American woman to do so, was similarly subject to excessive gate-keeping.[57] Her page was created in 2018 by Jess Wade as part of her efforts to make Wikipedia more equitable particularly in STEM subjects, but it was deleted five months later following a collective decision that Phelps was not notable.[58] Phelps' page was finally restored in 2020, but only after further interminable deliberations over her achievements and perceived shortcomings.[59]

The disproportionate scrutiny that Strickland and Phelps were subject to reflects how female subjects more generally are perceived and represented on Wikipedia, and notability has been turned into a question to decide the worth of women classicists by pile-on peer-review. The page for Eva Mroczek, a scholar of ancient Judaism, was tagged for deletion as not notable in 2020.[60] The survival of the page was decided only after lengthy discussions of her achievements and influence, with no accountability for those judging.[61] Despite the evident notability of Jinyu Liu, an expert on Roman history and the reception of Graeco-Roman classics in China, her page was nominated for deletion, again on the grounds of a lack of notability, less than a month after it was created.[62] The page was preserved but at the cost of more physical and emotional labour demanded in response to the pattern of hostility against women on Wikipedia rooted in racism and misogyny. The lack of regulatory oversight beyond Wikipedia's editing community itself makes this labour more demanding and challenging.

Nominating an article for deletion is a good way, but not the only way, to undermine women online. Disproportionate gate-keeping prevents pages from making it past the draft stage and being created, as demonstrated by so-far failed attempts to write Lisa Kallet, an ancient historian, and Mary Whitby, an expert of late antique Greek literature, into Wikipedia.[63] Pages for women can be easily reduced in quality and usefulness by disruptive editing and vandalism, such as the unexplained removal of sections of the page by anonymous editors. This is illustrated by edits made to the pages for the historical scholars Anna Julia Cooper, a hugely significant figure in African-American history and a Classics teacher, and Alice Zimmern, a Jewish Classicist and Suffragist.[64] Editors can attempt to resolve problems on pages as they perceive them, or they can 'tag' them with various notices that advertise them as substandard. Unfounded attempts to remove considerable sections of the page for Katherine Harloe following its tagging for violating copyright would have effectively ruined the page if they had not been reverted.[65] The aggressive policing of pages for women and the editors that contribute to them is demonstrated by the irate reaction to Dorothy Tarrant being described as professor emerita rather than emeritus, as recorded on the article's Talk Page.[66]

Comparing Wikipedia pages for men and women even in their numbers is a false equivalence; pages for men do not receive the same level of scrutiny or harassment as pages for non-binary people and women, particularly women of colour. Because of the controversial and conspicuous nature of their subjects, it would be reasonable to assume that pages for male classicists who have a history of harassment or sexual crimes would attract significant hostile attention. Instead, these pages become stamping grounds for different kinds of conflicts, primarily to control the narrative, minimising and effacing harms. The harms perpetrated on Wikipedia in the himpathetic erasure of uncomfortable aspects of male biographies, and the abuse and erasure of women, are linked beyond page histories.[67]

In the past decade, essential reflections have taken place in the field of Classics: what it is, why it is important, and who is included.[68] These were precipitated by #MeToo and Black Lives Matter, social change movements that drew on long traditions of feminist and antiracist resistance, lending prominence to reproductive rights, trans rights, and environmental justice.[69] Conversations between individuals, groups, and institutions about discrimination, oppression, and inequality in Classics are making these topics increasingly difficult to ignore. Whilst progress is far from even or joined up, and there is no guarantee against reversals, it would be difficult to envisage a return to previous ways of working and thinking that marginalised issues of equality.

There are no clear solutions to the systematic marginalisation and intersectional bias that this chapter has brought to the foreground. Yet targeted activism like #WCCWiki is successful in challenging Wikipedia's intractable gender bias from the inside and shifting online environments towards equity, inclusion, and representation, rather than platforms to perpetrate abuse, challenge, and exclusion. In choosing to assemble for each other, creating a new model of solidarity and affiliation, initiatives like #WCCWiki make Classics a publicly engaged discipline through a commitment to education and ethical knowledge-making, demonstrating that equality and excellence go together.

Notes

* I gratefully acknowledge the generous feedback of my readers Blossom Stefaniw, Mathura Umachandran, and Kate Cooper, which greatly improved the article.
1 See https://en.wikipedia.org/wiki/Edith_Morley (accessed 8 December 2021).

2   Morley (2016, 116–17). Despite Morley's stubborn refusal to accept her employer's unjust treatment, she internalised the sexist and misogynistic discrimination that was perpetrated against her: '…I have always been painfully conscious that my chair would be abolished when I reached the statutory age, and I have always worked with the unpleasant conviction that the necessary cost must outweigh the value of any service I could render the place whose interests I had at heart. It was a galling and unhappy result of my insistence on my position and one which I could never forget.' 117.
3   Royal Historical Society (2018, 8). See https://en.wikipedia.org/wiki/Katherine_Harloe. Last accessed 8 December 2021.
4   See https://en.wikipedia.org/wiki/Olivette_Otele (accessed 8 December 2021).
5   See https://www.bbc.com/afrique/region-45956066. https://www.bbc.co.uk/news/uk-46247776 (accessed 26 November, 2021).
6   Qureshi (2018).
7   Criado Perez (2016).
8   English Heritage 'Six New Blue Plaques for Women in 2020', 4 March 2020. https://www.english-heritage.org.uk/about-us/search-news/six-new-blue-plaques-for-women/ (accessed December 2021).
9   Thomas et al. (2021).
10 Institute for Government, 'Gender Balance in Parliament', https://www.instituteforgovernment.org.uk/publication/gender/parliament (accessed 8 December 2021).
11 Royal Society, *Diversity Data Report 2020*, 10. In 2020, 10% (152 individuals) of Fellows were female and 90% (1,362 individuals) were male. This proportion is unchanged from 2019.
12 According to data gather by the Higher Education Statistics Agency 2019/20. The proportion of women professors has increased by 1% point year on year since 2013/14. HESA, 'Higher Education Staff Statistics: UK, 2019/20', 19 January 2021. https://www.hesa.ac.uk/news/19-01-2021/sb259-higher-education-staff-statistics (accessed 8 December 2021).
13 HESA, 'Higher Education Staff Statistics: UK, 2019/20', 19 January 2021. https://www.hesa.ac.uk/news/19-01-2021/sb259-higher-education-staff-statistics (accessed 8 December 2021).
14 This is the *Times Higher Education World University Rankings* classification of a 'top university.' See https://www.timeshighereducation.com/news/one-fifth-worlds-top-universities-led-women (accessed 8 December 2021).
15 These roles are classified by HESA as classified as 'managers, directors and senior officials.' https://www.hesa.ac.uk/data-and-analysis/staff/table-3 (accessed 8 December 2021).
16 Williams et al. (2019, 3).
17 UKRI, 'Detailed Ethnicity Analysis of Funding Applicants and Awardees 2015–16 to 2019–20', 2020. See here: https://www.ukri.org/news/ukri-publishes-ethnicity-analysis-of-funding-applicants-and-awardees/ (accessed 8 December 2021).
18 The disproportionate burdening of women with caring work within higher education institutions is well known. Women are more concentrated in teaching roles and assume more emotional labour within academic

departments, including pastoral care and mentoring. For further discussion, see Morley (1999); Probert (2005); Grummell et al. (2009); Macfarlane and Burg (2019); Gaudet et al. (2022).
19 In 2018, the first official gender pay gap data collection showed that women in UK universities were paid a mean hourly wage that was almost 16% lower than their male colleagues, on average. Analysis in 2019 showed it had changed little, at 15%. See https://www.timeshighereducation.com/news/gender-pay-gap-uk-universities-report-slow-progress (accessed 8 December 2021).
20 Hill Collins (2014, 23).
21 Leonard and Lovatt (2020, 38–42).
22 Kelly et al. (2019) 442.
23 Leonard and Lovatt (2020, 35–6). It is likely that there will be a significant gender gap in journal submissions and peer review in Classics during the Covid-19 pandemic, with men receiving a cumulative advantage. See Gewin (2020) and Squazzoni et al. (2021).
24 In this volume, Samuel Agbamu articulates the unique relationship Classics has with nationalism and colonialism and compares how other disciplines based in the Humanities have confronted racial biases.
25 Heidi Safia Mirza (2018, 175) identifies a pernicious discourse of 'white hurt' that 'accompanies the multicultural backlash' and 'sees equality for people of colour as an unfair advantage rooted in political correctness.'
26 For more on institutional equality and diversity policies, see Ahmed (2012, 113–40).
27 Lerner (1986, 220).
28 Lerner (1986, 223).
29 For further discussion of the stereotyped assumptions modern scholars project onto the past, see Bennett (2006, 43).
30 Tripodi (2021).
31 Article totals: https://en.wikipedia.org/wiki/Wikipedia:Statistics. Page views: https://stats.wikimedia.org/#/all-projects (accessed 8 December 2021).
32 See https://www.alexa.com/topsites (accessed 8 December 2021).
33 See https://en.wikipedia.org/wiki/Instant_answer (accessed 8 December 2021).
34 See https://en.wikipedia.org/wiki/Gender_bias_on_Wikipedia (accessed 8 December 2021).
35 Nevell (2018) https://richardthecastellan.wordpress.com/2018/12/14/how-many-biographies-of-classicists-does-wikipedia-have/ (accessed 8 December 2021). For further discussion, see Leonard and Bond (2019).
36 Carruthers et al. (2021).
37 The Women's Classical Committee defines both 'women' and 'Classics' inclusively. See https://wcc-uk.blogs.sas.ac.uk/. For more information about #WCCWiki, see the Project Page: https://en.wikipedia.org/wiki/Wikipedia:Women%27s_Classical_Committee (accessed 8 December 2021).
38 For the full aims of the WCC, see here: https://wcc-uk.blogs.sas.ac.uk/ (accessed 13 April 2022).

39 Similar activist work that seeks to foreground women in classics includes Claire Catenaccio's *'Women in Classics: Conversations.'* See https://classicalstudies.org/blogs/claire-catenaccio (accessed 13 April 2022).
40 See Miriam T. Griffin: https://en.wikipedia.org/wiki/Miriam_T._Griffin; Annie Ure: https://en.wikipedia.org/wiki/Annie_Ure; Gillian Clark: https://en.wikipedia.org/wiki/Gillian_Clark_(historian); Leslie Brubaker: https://en.wikipedia.org/wiki/Leslie_Brubaker (accessed 8 December 2021). For the official record of #WCCWiki pages created and edited, which is likely to be a substantial undercount, see here: https://en.wikipedia.org/wiki/Wikipedia:Women%27s_Classical_Committee/Aims (accessed 13 April 2022).
41 The pages for Beryl Rawson, Grace Macurdy, Amy Richlin, Susanna Elm, and Semni Karouzou have all featured on Wikipedia's front page.
42 Wikipedia pages for Anna Apostolaki, Jacquetta Hawkes, Grace Macurdy, Semni Karouzou, Winifred Lamb, and Elizabeth Hazelton Haight have been designated as 'Good Articles.'
43 Nevell (2021) https://richardthecastellan.wordpress.com/2019/12/06/how-many-biographies-of-classicists-does-wikipedia-have-december-2019-update/ (accessed 8 December 2021).
44 Nevell (2019) https://richardthecastellan.wordpress.com/2019/12/06/how-many-biographies-of-classicists-does-wikipedia-have-december-2019-update/ (accessed 8 December 2021).
45 Although English language does predominate, where possible #WCCWiki is committed to editing and making pages in languages besides English, including for the French and German Wikipedias. For example, the page for Frazelia Campbell in German, created by Lucy Moore: https://de.wikipedia.org/wiki/Frazelia_Campbell (accessed 8 December 2021).
46 See the Wikidata Redlist: https://en.wikipedia.org/wiki/Wikipedia:Women%27s_Classical_Committee/Wikidata_redlist. For the crowd-sourced list, see here: https://en.wikipedia.org/wiki/Wikipedia:Women%27s_Classical_Committee/Aims#Women_working_in_Classics (accessed 8 December 2021).
47 European Women's Lobby, #HerNetHerRights. *Resource Page on Ending Online Violence Against Women and Girls in Europe*, 2017. Amnesty International, 'Troll Patrol Findings. Using Crowdsourcing, Data Science and Machine Learning to Measure Violence and Abuse Against Women on Twitter' (2018) (accessed 8 December 2021).
48 See https://en.wikipedia.org/wiki/Gender_bias_on_Wikipedia (accessed 8 December 2021).
49 Tripodi (2021).
50 See https://en.wikipedia.org/wiki/Donna_Zuckerberg (accessed 8 December 2021).
51 See https://en.wikipedia.org/wiki/Priyamvada_Gopal. https://en.wikipedia.org/wiki/Mary_Beard_(classicist) (accessed 8 December 2021).
52 See https://en.wikipedia.org/wiki/Ivory_Bangle_Lady (accessed 8 December 2021).
53 See https://en.wikipedia.org/wiki/Wikipedia:Notability and https://en.wikipedia.org/wiki/Wikipedia:Notability_(academics) (accessed 8 December 2021).
54 See https://en.wikipedia.org/wiki/Donna_Strickland (accessed 8 December 2021).

55 See https://en.wikipedia.org/w/index.php?title=Donna_Strickland&dir=prev&limit=500&action=history (accessed 8 December 2021). Tripodi (2021).
56 See https://en.wikipedia.org/wiki/Talk:Donna_Strickland. https://en.wikipedia.org/wiki/Talk:Donna_Strickland/Archive_1#Material_on_AfC_rejection (accessed 8 December 2021).
57 See https://en.wikipedia.org/wiki/Clarice_Phelps (accessed 8 December 2021).
58 See https://thewire.in/science/what-a-deleted-profile-tells-us-about-wikipedias-diversity-problem (accessed 8 December 2021).
59 See https://en.wikipedia.org/wiki/Wikipedia:Deletion_review/Log/2019_May_1#Clarice_Phelps/. https://en.wikipedia.org/wiki/Wikipedia:Articles_for_deletion/Clarice_Phelps_(2nd_nomination) (accessed 8 December 2021).
60 See https://en.wikipedia.org/wiki/Eva_Mroczek (accessed 8 December 2021).
61 See https://en.wikipedia.org/wiki/Wikipedia:Articles_for_deletion/Eva_Mroczek (accessed 8 December 2021).
62 See https://en.wikipedia.org/wiki/Jinyu_Liu. https://en.wikipedia.org/wiki/Wikipedia:Articles_for_deletion/Jinyu_Liu (accessed 8 December 2021).
63 Mary Whitby is represented on Wikidata only: https://www.wikidata.org/wiki/Q87401966 (accessed 8 December 2021).
64 See https://en.wikipedia.org/wiki/Alice_Zimmern (accessed 8 December 2021). https://en.wikipedia.org/w/index.php?title=Alice_Zimmern&curid=31296576&diff=1058185855&oldid=1058174385 (accessed 8 December 2021).
65 See https://en.wikipedia.org/w/index.php?title=Katherine_Harloe&diff=914524436&oldid=914515809 (accessed 8 December 2021).
66 See https://en.wikipedia.org/wiki/Talk:Dorothy_Tarrant (accessed 8 December 2021).
67 Philosopher Kate Manne understands 'himpathy' as the disproportionate sympathy powerful men receive in cases of sexual assault, intimate partner violence, homicide, and other misogynistic behaviour. For discussion, see Manne (2018, 196–205).
68 Chae (2018); Padilla Peralta (2019).
69 Shahmima Akhtar (2021) discusses this global shift and contextualises it within the discipline of History.

Works Cited

Ahmed, S. (2012) *On Being Included: Racism and Diversity in Institutional Life*, Durham, NC.

Akhtar, S. (2021) 'Revisiting RHS's 'Race, Ethnicity and Equality in UK History: A Report and Resource for Change', *Royal Historical Society Transactions* 31: 116–18.

Bennett, J.M. (2006) *History Matters. Patriarchy and the Challenge of Feminism*, Manchester.

Carruthers, W., Niala, J., Davis, S., Challis, D., Schiappacasse, P.A., Dixon, S., Milosavljević, M., Moore, L., Nevell, R., Fitzpatrick, A., Abd el Gawad,

H. and Stevenson, A. (2021) 'Special Issue: Inequality and Race in the Histories of Archaeology', *Bulletin of the History of Archaeology* 31: 4.

Chae, Y. (2018) 'White People Explain Classics to Us', *Eidolon*, 5 February.

Criado Perez, C. (2016) 'I Sorted the UK's Statues by Gender—a Mere 2.7 Per Cent Are of Historical, Non-Royal Women', *New Statesmen*, 26 March.

Gaudet, S., Marchand, I., Bujaki, M. and Bourgeault, I.L. (2022) 'Women and Gender Equity in Academia Through the Conceptual Lens of Care', *Journal of Gender Studies* 31: 74–86.

Gewin, V. (2020) 'The Career Cost of COVID-19 to Female Researchers, and How Science Should Respond', *Nature* 583: 867–9.

Grummell, B., Devine, D. and Lynch, K. (2009) 'The Care-less Manager: Gender, Care and New Managerialism in Higher Education', *Gender and Education* 21: 191–208.

Hill Collins, P. (2014) *Black Feminist Thought: Knowledge, Consciousness, and the Politics of Empowerment*, London.

Kelly, C. et al. (2019) 'Gender Bias and the Journal of Roman Studies', *Journal of Roman Studies* 109: 441–8.

Leonard, V. and Bond, S.E. (2019) 'Advancing Feminism Online: Online Tools, Visibility, and Women in Classics', *Studies in Late Antiquity* 3.1: 4–16.

Leonard, V. and Lovatt, H. (2020) 'Council of University Classical Departments Equality and Diversity Report 2020', *CUCD EDI Blog*, 1–76.

Lerner, G. (1986) *The Creation of the Patriarchy*, Oxford.

Macfarlane, B. and Burg, D. (2019) 'Women Professors and the Academic Housework Trap', *Journal of Higher Education Policy and Management* 41: 262–74.

Manne, K. (2018) *Down Girl: The Logic of Misogyny*, Oxford.

Mirza, H.S. (2018) 'Black Bodies 'Out of Place' in Academic Spaces: Gender, Race, Faith and Culture in Post-Race Times', in J. Arday and H.S. Mirza (eds) *Dismantling Race in Higher Education, Racism, Whiteness and Decolonising the Academy*, London.

Morley, E. (2016) *Before and After. Reminiscences of a Working Life*, Reading.

Morley, L. (1999) *Organising Feminisms: The Micropolitics of the Academy*, Basingstoke.

Nevell, R. (2018) 'How Many Biographies of Classicists does Wikipedia Have?', 14 December, https://richardthecastellan.wordpress.com/2018/12/14/how-many-biographies-of-classicists-does-wikipedia-have/

Nevell, R. (2019) 'How Many Biographies of Classicists does Wikipedia Have? December 2019 Update', 6 December, https://richardthecastellan.wordpress.com/2019/12/06/how-many-biographies-of-classicists-does-wikipedia-have-december-2019-update/

Nevell, R. (2021) 'How Many Biographies of Classicists does Wikipedia Have? July 2021 Update', 28 July, https://richardthecastellan.wordpress.com/2019/12/06/how-many-biographies-of-classicists-does-wikipedia-have-december-2019-update/

Padilla Peralta, D. (2019) 'Some Thoughts on AIA-SCS 2019', *Medium*, 7 January.
Probert, B. (2005) '"I Just Couldn't Fit In": Gender and Unequal Outcomes in Academic Careers', *Gender, Work and Organization* 12: 50–72.
Qureshi, S. (2018) 'Black History', *London Review of Books* 40.22, 22 November.
Royal Historical Society (2018) *Race, Ethnicity and Equality in UK History: A Report and Resource for Change*, 1–122.
Squazzoni, F., Bravo, G., Grimaldo, F., García-Costa, D., Farjam, M. and Mehmani, B. (2021) 'Gender Gap in Journal Submissions and Peer Review During the First Wave of the COVID-19 Pandemic. A Study on 2329 Elsevier Journals', *PLoS ONE* 16.10: e0257919.
Thomas, T., Mohdin, A. and Duncan, P. (2021) 'Only 2% of Blue Plaques in London Commemorate Black people', *The Guardian*, 5 October.
Tripodi, F. (2021) 'Ms. Categorized: Gender, Notability, and Inequality on Wikipedia', *New Media and Society*.
Williams, P., Bath, S., Arday, J. and Lewis, C. (2019) 'The Broken Pipeline – Barriers to Black PhD Students Accessing Research Council Funding', *Leading Routes*, 1–8.

7 'Biting the Hand that Feeds You?'
Responding to Racialisation in UK Classics

Samuel Agbamu

> To establish his own identity, Caliban [...] must himself pioneer into regions Caesar never knew.
>
> C. L. R. James, Beyond a Boundary[1]

So wrote the Trinidadian Marxist intellectual in his work *Beyond a Boundary*, ostensibly a book about cricket but a wide-ranging study of the relation between culture, colonialism, and identity. In some ways, James' wrestling with his anti-colonialism and his own eurocentrism emblematises my relationship towards the discipline in which I am embedded. When I tell people that I am a classicist, they frequently express surprise.[2] I can hardly blame them. For laypeople in the UK, the idea of classics conjures up images of Boris Johnson, mumbling something about immigration and the fall of the Roman Empire,[3] dusty tomes, and ivory towers. For some, Enoch Powell's allusions to the *Aeneid* in his notorious 1968 'Rivers of Blood' speech may even be a point of reference.[4] What, then, does someone of mixed Nigerian, Bangladeshi, and English heritage (and a Muslim, to boot) have to do with a discipline with such a dubious pedigree? In response to such questions, I often go for the easy option and say that I enjoyed languages, literature, and history at school, so classics seemed like the obvious choice. However, if I am honest with myself and with my interlocutors, it is a bit more complicated than that.

Biting the Hand that Feeds

My relation to classics can partly be explained with reference to another product of empire enamoured with the worlds of classical antiquity: Cyril Lionel Robert (C.L.R.) James (1901–1989). James was a Trinidadian, Marxist intellectual and activist, perhaps best-known today for his ground-breaking history of the Haitian Revolution,

DOI: 10.4324/9781003278016-8

The Black Jacobins (1938, 2nd ed. 1963). His career spanned the Atlantic and a dazzling array of literary forms, from sports writing to tragedy, novels to anthropology, yet throughout his cultural and political outputs, the classical tradition maintains a strong presence.[5] This was, James explains in his autobiographical writings, partly due to his education. As a young boy, he won an exhibition at the prestigious Queen's Royal College, in Port of Spain, Trinidad, and Tobago, a school closely modelled on the Arnoldian English Public School. Of his studies, James writes, 'I began to study Latin and French, then Greek, and much else,' spending eight years learning Latin with Virgil, Caesar, and Horace, and Greek with Thucydides and Euripides. The result of this was James seeing himself as a 'British intellectual' before the age of ten, 'an alien' in his own environment and among his own family.[6]

In the mid-1930s, James, now living in England, became a committed and active anti-imperialist and communist, an attitude galvanised, in part, by the Fascist Italian invasion of Abyssinia in 1935. In the context of this decisive turn to anticolonial politics, James saw his colonial education in a new light. In an article on 'Abyssinia and the Imperialists' for the journal of the League of Coloured Peoples, *The Keys*, James wrote:

> Africans and people of African descent, especially those who have been poisoned by British imperialist education, needed a lesson. They have got it. Every succeeding day shows exactly the real motives which move imperialism in its contact with Africa, shows the incredible savagery and duplicity of European imperialism in its quest for markets and raw materials. Let the lesson sink in deep.[7]

James began to increasingly draw on his classical education in order to articulate his anticolonial, antiracist, and socialist politics.[8] This drew ire from all sides, with Derek Walcott, for example, responding to James' book on cricket, *Beyond a Boundary*, as follows:

> Mr. James's ancestors are African; why does he find mimesis in Periclean and not African sculpture when he describes the grace of his cricketers?[9]

On the other hand, James received racist letters, such as this one below, sent to the *International African Opinion*, the journal of the International African Service Bureau for whom James wrote:

> It is only from the rulers whom you so hate that you have received the education that has enabled you to bite the hand that feeds you.[10]

James responded:

> As far as we know, it is to the Babylonians, the Egyptians, the Jews, and the Greeks that Europe owes the foundations of its culture. The Arabs contributed heavily during the Middle Ages. But we have not noticed any special feeling of gratitude among the modern Europeans either to Arab or Jew, for instance.[11]

For James, then, his British colonial education, with a heavy emphasis on 'the best that has been thought and said in the world,'[12] provided tools with which to construct an anticolonial politics. At the same time, recourse to the cultures of Greece and Rome, but especially Greece, to which James had as valid a claim as any white European, allowed him to give voice to what he saw as the hybridity of European cultures, which owed much to the peoples of Africa and Asia, 'Arab' and 'Jew.' Half a century later, Martin Bernal's *Black Athena* (vol. 1, 1987) would make similar claims, attracting hostile responses from the classical establishment.[13] However, as with his Toussaint Louverture in *Black Jacobins*, attempting to formulate an anticolonial politics in the language of a colonial modernity, underpinned by a reverence for classical antiquity, ultimately led James to a crossroad with no clear direction to take.[14]

I begin with James because my journey through a classical education in some way shadows his. My initial steps into classics were motivated by a genuine, albeit unreflexive, interest in the texts and material cultures of ancient Greece and Rome. I used to feel very clever when arguing that studying dead languages was important because the Greeks and the Roman shaped who 'we' are today—from *our* political institutions to *our* scientific knowledge, *our* literature to *our* architecture.

I suppose also that, on a subconscious level, I thought that studying classics might give me access to the essence of Britishness. Despite being born in the UK, despite my middle-class background, and despite not being able to speak any of my family's mother tongues (apart from that of my Liverpudlian grandmother), my relationship to my nationality is strained. Roughly when I was choosing my GCSEs—the exams taken mostly between the ages of 15 and 16—up to going to study classics at university, the British National Party was on the ascendency.

Nick Griffin, the leader of the party, was invited onto *Question Time*, the BBC topical debate, in 2009 and, in the same year, was elected as a Member of the European Parliament. Not to say that there was no racism in my school prior to this renaissance of the racist right—partly a reaction, I suppose, to the perceived failure of the project of Blairite multiculturalism as well as the increasing prominence of the threat of Islamist terrorism in discourses of national security, particularly after the 7/7 bombings—but I certainly became more aware of the pervasiveness of racist attitudes in the run-up to sitting my A-Levels, the school-leaving qualifications, generally taken between the ages of 17 and 18. I remember the frequency with which the term 'freshie' (short for 'fresh off the boat' – i.e., a recent immigrant) was directed at those particularly from South Asian backgrounds, as well as it being used within these groups, variably as a term of affection or ridicule. Phiroze Vasunia has shown the pervasiveness of the valorisation of classical education in the British colonial administration in the Indian subcontinent, and Barbara Goff has similarly demonstrated the prestige held by the classics in West Africa, where Greek and Latin were seen as the 'secret language' of the colonial elites.[15] In defence of my mid-teen self, then, it would seem only reasonable that I might seek to assert my belonging as a Briton—to demonstrate that not only was I not 'fresh off the boat,' but that I had never been on the boat—through the pursuit of the same sort of education that allowed James to see himself as a 'British intellectual.'

Imagine my thrill, then, when I learned about the so-called 'Orientalising Revolution,' or about the fact that there were Africans in Roman Britain. As I became increasingly aware of the uses of Greece and Rome in white supremacist discourse, what better rebuttal, I thought, to racist claims of European exceptionalism than to point out that, for example, the Pythagoras Theorem was in use by the Babylonians centuries before Pythagoras was born, or that the Greek alphabet in which Homer's epics were transcribed was developed from the Phoenician? What more persuasive response to the claim that 'there ain't no black in the Union Jack' than revising upwards Peter Fryer's famous assertion that 'Black people – by whom [he] mean[s] Africans and Asians and their descendants – have been living in Britain for close on 500 years' to 2000 years?[16]

But, of course, this is not enough. There is little use in asserting the worthiness of cultural identities only insofar as they relate to 'European civilisation' other than serving to reinforce the classical tradition as the measure and arbiter of 'civilisation.' Would the presence of Black people in the UK be less legitimate if the first immigrant from

Africa, Asia, or the Caribbean had only arrived last week? Or would the cultures of the Near and Middle East be less worthy of respect if they had not contributed to the foundations of literacy and geometry in the ancient Mediterranean? In other words, I slowly moved away from trying to fit myself *around* what I read about classical antiquity and began instead to put myself *into* what I read about it.

Are You Afraid of the Dark?

By no means am I even close to being the first classicist of colour to seek to put myself into my research. Shelley Haley led the way with a series of publications, beginning in the late 1980s, in applying methods drawn from the burgeoning analytical frameworks of Critical Race Studies and Intersectionality to the study of the ancient Mediterranean.[17] In one of these contributions, 'Black Feminist Thought and Classics,' Haley explicitly draws on her own experiences in order to elaborate her responses to the literature and material culture of the ancient Mediterranean. However, both 'Black Feminist Thought' and the later, 'Be Not Afraid of the Dark,' memorable, for me, through its masterful comparison of translations of Pseudo-Virgils' *Moretum*, appeared in edited volumes dedicated to investigating Feminist approaches to antiquity, or race, ethnicity, and gender in classical and biblical antiquity, rather than in high-ranking peer-reviewed journals. This is not, of course, to say that leading Anglophone classics journals are not publishing excellent work on race, ethnicity, and gender in the ancient Mediterranean and the implication of these approaches for the discipline as a whole. I look, in particular, to 2023 special issues of *Transactions of the American Philological Society*, on race and racism, edited by Patrice Rankine and Sarah-Mae Eccleston.

However, in many respects, classics, as a discipline, lags behind other fields of the humanities. In recent years, there have been a series of publications on Premodern Critical Race Studies coming out of Medieval and Early Modern Studies contexts that have given me, as a classicist, a lot to think about. Given the 'middle-ness' of the Middle Ages, Medieval Critical Race scholars have wrestled with the implications of race and periodisation to a greater extent than I have seen done by scholars working on race in antiquity.[18]

I think it is more-or-less taken for granted that classical antiquity roughly spans the period between Homer and Hesiod, possibly earlier into Minoan and Mycenaean cultures, up to the fall of the Western Roman Empire, whenever you think that is. If classics is the study of ancient Greece and Rome, its texts, material cultures, and their reception, then what would it mean to extend 'classical antiquity' up to 1453 and the fall of Byzantium? Many scholars of Byzantium, up to 1453 and beyond, are based in classics departments, but I am speaking of Byzantine studies not being an appendage of classics, but a core element of it. This would force classics to reckon with, not only a more thorough appraisal of 'post-classical' migrations across Europe, but also the interactions between the Latin West, Greek East, and Muslim worlds. Islamic expansion, after all, has been seen as contributing to the decline of the Roman world by important scholars of late antiquity so it would make sense to learn something about Islam in classics departments.[19] Such reappraisals of periodisation would have radical consequences for the teaching and study of classical antiquity, and while this may be a conversation that does not go anywhere, it would still be a conversation worth having. As Nicole Lopez-Jantzen, a scholar of late antique and early modern Italy writes:

> conceptualizing and teaching multiple ways of dividing up the past not only serves as a potential challenge to the master narrative and its refinements, but also sheds light on the multiple ways people may have experienced the past.[20]

Thus, not only has engaging with scholarship on the periodisation of the Middle Ages forced me to reconsider the stakes of not taking 'classical antiquity' for granted, but it has also shown me ways in which I can articulate my subjectivity in my research.

A recent issue of *Literature Compass* was based on proceedings from the 2019 RaceB4Race symposium at Arizona State University. RaceB4Race, a collaboration between the US-based Medievalists of Colour and Shakespeare and Race networks, has since organised a series of events, approaching Premodern Critical Race Studies from a number of perspectives. In this issue of *Literature Compass*, Shakoofeh Rajabzadeh wrote about the implicitly embodied whiteness of Medieval Studies, but much of what is written here is very applicable to classics. Rajabzadeh had previously written about the erasure of Muslims and the figure of the Saracen in Medieval texts.[21] Later, in the 'Premodern Critical Race Studies' special issue of *Literature Compass*, Rajabzadeh, reflecting on the influence of her positionality on her scholarship, writes:

> The Middle Ages that I think about and write about is one that is processed through me. In this Middle Ages, nothing that affects how I am in the world is deemed anachronistic because

the theoretical, political, social, and legal forces that govern how I operate in the world are the ones that affect how and what I know about history, how and what I think about space.[22]

The clarity of this articulation of the relationship between identity and scholarship gives me much to consider in how I approach my own research, which broadly concerns the role of classical, especially Roman antiquity, in the formulation of early modern and modern ideas of race, nation, and empire. I do not want to give the impression that classics is ignoring such issues as articulated by Rajabzadeh. Indeed, classicists are very much a part of such conversations, and there are a number of great networks of classicists in the US which explore questions of race in antiquity and modernity, for example, Eos Africana, the Asian and Asian American Classical Caucus, and more recently, Hesperides.[23] However, there are no national networks on the scale of these, Medievalists of Colour, or ShakeRace in UK classics and Medieval Studies.[24]

Yet, despite the recent proliferation of such exciting work on race and ethnicity in premodernity, serious obstacles remain, hindering racialised scholars in classics and adjacent fields from 'putting themselves into' their research. The Princeton classicist Dan-el Padilla Peralta became the centre of controversy with a presentation on the 'Future of Classics' at the 2019 annual meeting of the US-based Society for Classical Studies, the world's largest professional association for classicists. In this presentation, Padilla Peralta presents 20-years' worth of demographic data relating to authors publishing in three leading North American classics journals.[25] In terms of gender-based and race-based imbalance of who is being published, the picture painted by Padilla Peralta is stark. Of course, the minority of people of colour in North American classics departments and PhD programmes goes a long way to explaining these vast discrepancies in publication, but this itself poses serious questions for the future of an equitable discipline in the USA and Canada. In order to 'recognize, honor, and repair the silencing of the knowledge that people of color carry,' Padilla Peralta suggests that 'holders of privilege will need to surrender their privilege.'[26] The concrete implications of this in an 'an economy of academic prestige defined and governed by scarcity,'[27] provoked impassioned responses from both sides of the Atlantic.

For example, the German ancient historian, Stefan Rebenich characterises Padilla Peralta intervention as 'reverse racism,' and an attack on the principle of double-blind peer review. In closing, Rebenich mentions an open letter signed by 200 students of the Classics faculty at Oxford, demanding compulsory racial bias training for staff. Rebenich refers also to what he sees as 'a preferential path to be offered to "people of colour" to obtain a place [of study]' in the students' demands.[28] It is striking that responses to Padilla Peralta should both note the dominance of voices of scholars from the USA when it comes to conversations around race and classics,[29] but also critique anti-racist initiatives in classics departments in the UK.[30] The question then remains, what does 'reverse racism' of 'Equality, Diversity, and Inclusivity' initiatives in UK classics HE looks like?

Against Diversity?

In November 2020, the Council of University Classics Departments, 'the professional forum for all teachers of classical Greek and Roman subjects in British Universities,' published a report on *Equality and Diversity in Classics*, written by Victoria Leonard (Royal Holloway, University of London) and Helen Lovatt (University of Nottingham). The findings—discussed also by Leonard in this volume—provide salutary, if not totally unpredictable, reading. Results drawn from two surveys, the Experience Survey and the Departmental Contexts Survey, highlight the prevalence of gender-based biases and discrimination, and shows that discrimination on the basis of gender is the most frequently reported among respondents.[31] The report also underlines the relative lack of visibility of BAME (Black and Minority Ethnic) classicists in leadership roles and in prestigious fellowship. Only 8.1% of respondents were BAME, compared with 15.1% of the UK population, according to the 2011 national census.[32] The report also presents data on publication in three prestigious UK classics journals: *Classical Quarterly*; *The Journal of Roman Studies*; and *The Journal of Hellenic Studies*. Women and non-binary scholars, and those from BAME backgrounds are less likely to submit work to these journals due to 'health reasons, caring responsibilities and teaching workloads,' or because they felt that 'their research would not be suitable or 'a good fit,' or that publishing there would be unattainable.'[33] Respondents also consider these journals as uninterested in Reception Studies and publishing only a 'type' of scholar from which respondents see themselves as deviating. This is a finding which was earlier articulated by Mathura Umachandran:

> That Classics is still—at all levels—constituted overwhelmingly by a white majority, is not simply a coincidence. It is a political

reality that asserts again and again that the privilege of inquiry into the past is the guarded by a line of colour.[34]

This bears further thought since, if UK HE classics rightly sees it as a priority to improve equality and diversity practices in hiring processes, 'diverse' hires are being set up to fail in the 'economy of academic prestige' described by Padilla Peralta.[35]

What then would diversity in UK classics HE looks like? In a core critique of institutionalised 'diversity,' Sara Ahmed underlines the fact that diversity work is unequally distributed, falling on the shoulders of 'diverse' colleagues who are subject to a double bind: 'if diversity and equality work is less valued by organisations, then to become responsible for this work can mean to inhabit institutional spaces that are also less valued'.[36] Citing Nirmal Puwar, Ahmed suggests that 'diversity,' by 'adding colour' to an organisation, reinscribes its normative whiteness. Workers of colour are welcomed into white institutions on the condition of their '"being" diverse.'[37] At the same time, when institutionalised diversity becomes subsumed into being a means to the end of the murky notion of institutional 'excellence,' 'diversity' becomes a symptom of the corporate university. If, then, 'diversity' is understood as an empty vessel, we can 'throw more things into it.'[38] As Ahmed suggests, it remains a useful prompt for important conversations:

> Diversity does not refer us to something (a shared object that exists around speech) or even necessarily create something that can be shared. But in being spoke, and repeated in different contexts, a world takes shape around diversity. To speak the language of diversity is to participate in the creation of a world.[39]

Classicists have something important to add to this discussion. The classicist Nandini Pandey's recent work explores the concept of 'diversity' in Roman antiquity. In some contexts, it assumes the guise of a tool of imperial domination. In his *On Agriculture* (1.17), Varro advises slave owners to maintain a diverse body of unfree labour to prevent clan-based infighting.[40] 'On some level,' Pandey reflects, 'the Romans knew that their success and very survival depended on their inclusiveness'.[41] Classics, as a discipline, needs to be 'diverse' and 'inclusive' in order to stay relevant in our globalised world. The question is whether an inclusive classic will be a tool of dominance or emancipation. In any case, centring reflexive work in classics—beyond special issues and edited volumes—should shake the academic economy of prestige to its core. Therefore, to quote C.L.R. James, to establish our own identities in classics, we Calibans must pioneer into regions Caesar never knew.

Notes

1. James (1980, 11).
2. Umachandran (2017) and Dhindsa (2020) have also written about their experience of the relationship between racial injustices and their studies in classics.
3. Walker (2021).
4. Discussed recently by Pandey (2021).
5. See Worcester (1992); Greenwood (2010, 188–235); Quest (2017).
6. James (1980, 26–28).
7. James (1992) 63.
8. For example, James (1956).
9. Walcott (1984), cit. Greenwood (2010, 196–197). Cf. discussions of this same point in the US Marxist journal *Correspondence* during the 1950s, cit. Quest (2017).
10. Cit. Gopal (2019) 336.
11. *Ibid.* 337.
12. Matthew Arnold, cit. Høgsbjerg (2014).
13. Perhaps most significantly, Lefkowitz (1996).
14. Scott (2004) describes James and Toussaint as 'conscripts of modernity'.
15. Vasunia (2013); Goff (2013).
16. Fryer (2018) xvii.
17. See, especially, Haley (1993), (2009).
18. See the 2021 special issue of *New Literary* History, 52:3.
19. For example, Pirenne (1937).
20. Lopez-Jantzen (2021, 270).
21. Rajabzadeh (2019).
22. Rajabzadeh (2021).
23. See https://www.eosafricana.org/; https://www.aaaclassicalcaucus.org/; https://www.hesperideslusohispano.org/
24. There are a number of local-/university-based groups for students and researchers of colour, lead mostly by undergraduate and postgraduate students, for example, the Christian Cole Society (Oxford) and London Classicists of Colour.
25. Padilla Peralta (2019).
26. Ibid. 7–8.
27. Ibid.
28. Rebenich in Canfora (2021).
29. Ibid.
30. Ibid.
31. Leonard and Lovatt (2020, 19). See also Leonard, in this volume, on the presence of BAME and especially BAME women, among the professoriate of UK humanities.
32. Ibid. 8; 14.
33. Ibid. 34
34. Umachandran (2017).

35 Padilla Peralta (2019, 8).
36 Ahmed (2012) 4.
37 Ahmed (2012, 33, 43), citing Puwar (2004, 1).
38 Ahmed (2012, 80).
39 Ibid. 81.
40 Pandey (2020–2021).
41 Pandey (2018).

Works Cited

Ahmed, S. (2012) *On Being Included: Racism and Diversity in Institutional Life*, Durham, NC.
Canfora, L. (2021) 'Editoriale. I Classici "Decolonizzati"', *Quaderni Di Storia* 63: 5–11.
Dhindsa, H.S. (2020) 'What Studying Classics Taught Be About My Relationship With Western Civilisation', *CUCD Bulletin*, 49.
Fryer, P. (2018) *Staying Power: The History of Black People in Britain*, London.
Goff, B. (2013) *'Your Secret Language': Classics in the British Colonies of West Africa*, London.
Gopal, P. (2019) *Insurgent Empire: Anticolonial Resistance and British Dissent*, London.
Greenwood, E. (2010) *Afro-Greeks: Dialogues Between Anglophone Caribbean Literature and Classics in the Twentieth Century*, Oxford.
Haley, S.P. (1993) 'Black Feminist Thought and Classics: Re-Membering, Re-Claiming, Re-empowering', in N. Rabinowitz and A. Richlin (eds.), *Feminist Theory and the Classics*, London, 23–43.
Haley, S.P. (2009) 'Be Not Afraid of the Dark: Critical Race Theory and Classical Studies', in L. Nasrallah and E.S. Fiorenza (eds.), *Prejudice and Christian Beginnings*, Minneapolis, MN, 27–50.
Høgsbjerg, C.J. (2014) *C. L. R. James in Imperial Britain*, Durham, NC.
James, C.L.R. (1956) 'Every Cook Can Govern: A Study of Democracy in Ancient Greece and Its Meaning for Today', *Correspondence* 2: 12.
James, C.L.R. (1980 [1963]) *Beyond a Boundary*, London.
James, C.L.R. (1992) *The C.L.R. James Reader*, edited by A. Grimshaw, Oxford.
Lefkowitz, M. (1996) *Not Out of Africa: How Afrocentrism Became an Excuse to Teach Myth as History*, New York, NY.
Leonard, V. and Lovatt, H. (2020) 'Council of University Classical Departments Equality and Diversity Report 2020', *CUCD EDI Blog*, 1–76.
Lopez-Jantzen, N. (2021) 'Historiography, Periodization, and Race: Italy between Antiquity and the Middle Ages, Europe and Africa', *New Literary History* 52.3: 469–87.
Padilla Peralta, D. (2019) 'Racial Equity and the Production of Knowledge' [paper presentation], SCS 2019: The Future of Classics, San Diego, CA., USA, 5 January.

Pandey, N. (2018) 'Turning the Tables on Dominance and Diversity in Classics', *Eidolon*, 9 July.

Pandey, N. (2020) '–21) 'The Roman Roots of Racial Capitalism: What an Ancient Empire Can Teach Us About Diversity', *The Berlin Journal* 34: 16–20.

Pandey, N. (2021) 'The River Tiber, Foaming with Much Ink: Countering Anti-Immigrant Excerptions of the Aeneid' [paper presentation] Symposium Cumanum 2021: Identity in Virgil, Online, 26 June.

Pirenne, H. (1939) *Mohammed and Charlemagne*, London.

Puwar, N. (2004) *Space Invaders: Race, Gender and Bodies Out of Place*, Oxford.

Quest, M. (2017) 'Direct Democracy and the Search for Identity for Colonized People: the Contemporary Meanings of C.L.R. James's Classical Athens', *Classical Receptions Journal* 9.2: 237–67.

Rajabzadeh, S. (2019) 'The Depoliticized Saracen and Muslim Erasure', *Literature Compass* 16: e12548.

Rajabzadeh, S. (2021) 'The Intellectual Body, the Body Intellectual', *Literature Compass* 18.10: e12618.

Scott, D. (2004) *Conscripts of Modernity*, Durham, NC.

Umachandran, M. (2017) 'Fragile, Handle with Care. On White Classicists', *Eidolon*, 5 June.

Vasunia, P. (2013) *The Classics and Colonial India*, Oxford.

Walcott, D. (1984) 'A Classic of Cricket, a Legend of Baseball', *New York Times*, 25 March.

Walker, P. (2021) 'Cop26 Failure Could Mean Mass Migration and Food Shortages, Says Boris Johnson', *The Guardian*, 30 October.

Worcester, K. (1992) 'The Question of the Canon: C. L. R. James and Modern Politics', in P. Henry and P. Buhle (eds.), *P. C. L. R. James' Caribbean*, Durham, NC, 210–25.

8 Teaching Visual/Material Culture and Museums in Terms of Disability Access

Ellen Adams

This chapter focuses on the British context, where the Disability Discrimination Act (DDA) of 1995 obliged all public bodies, including museums, to make their services accessible to disabled people. This is relevant to other countries as well (for example, the 1990 Americans with Disability Act),[1] and the United Nations Convention on the Rights of Persons with Disabilities (CRPD) stands as a global statement on disability rights. The DDA includes duties for universities to adapt to students with disabilities. While this is best done on a case-by-case basis, the obligation is anticipatory, meaning that teachers should expect to cater for students with disabilities, rather than waiting to be notified and then responding appropriately. This has led to thinking about inclusive teaching, whereby the accessibility is present throughout the learning environment and may have benefits for *all* students. The process of making materials accessible involves thinking in depth about how we communicate and ways of learning. There is also the issue of representation. Given the tendency in HE disability services to assume that only students are likely to be disabled, pressure is placed on staff with invisible disabilities to mask them. There is therefore a lack of disabled role models in the sector, along with a tendency to view students solely as receivers of accessible content, rather than training them in the need to produce it as well.

Training Students in Accessibility

The Council for University Classical Departments (CUCD) Equality and Diversity Report, published in November 2020, focused primarily on race and gender, but Table 5 on Page 14 indicates that Postgraduates and teaching assistants were far more likely to declare a disability than Lecturer-Professors levels.[2] There are many reasons for this, including changing generational attitudes, with increasingly

DOI: 10.4324/9781003278016-9

less stigma to declaring a disability and less pressure to mask any impairments among younger people. Whether those in permanent lectureships are genuinely non-disabled or masking, this table paints a picture of few disabled role models. Universities are places of excellence, which traditionally implies high-functioning bodies and minds at their peak–hence the deep-rooted assumption that disability only concerns students, not staff. However, it should not be assumed that assignments do not need to be accessible. As educators, our attention may be first and foremost on making our materials accessible to students, but there is also the obligation to train them in generating accessible content themselves.

Innovative types of assessment now include e-portfolios and presentations for web/screen rather than traditional written essays. If students have been asked to produce digital assessment, then training in digital competency is necessary (and will be transferable skills for life and work beyond university). Any public-facing digital content should conform to accessibility requirements in a way not required for a standard written assessment. For example, going digital presents the obligation to provide a short description of visual material in the form of Alt Text. For video/spoken content, captions should be enabled, even if just automatically generated. Accessibility includes presentation, such as the use of sans serif fonts and clear colour contrast, and not placing text in front of noisy backgrounds, as this would confuse text-to-voice software. In Britain, digital services must meet level AA of the Web Content Accessibility Guidelines (WCAG 2.1) as a minimum;[3] this is therefore a basic standard for digital competency.

It would be good to see this practice influencing more traditional communication methods, such as PowerPoint presentations. It is still common to see a speaker rush through numerous visuals, without really pausing to explore what is being shown (the audience is assumed to have good vision, so they are expected to figure it out for themselves). It is also common for speakers to leave the audience to read text shown on a slide, while talking over it. Few non-disabled people can process two different sets of information simultaneously (we think we can multitask: we cannot), for neurodiverse people, or those with hearing or vision impairments, this challenge is likely to be unsurmountable. Being aware of this does not just make material more accessible, but it also improves communication for all, by making it clearer, simpler, and focusing on one medium at a time.

Teaching staff are stretched, and not necessarily equipped to train students in accessibility and digital student assessments, so we rely on the support of central IT specialists (known in my institution as

TEL—technology-enhanced learning support staff). My request for support to give guidance to students about how to make their work accessible appears to have been the first of its kind in my institution, and there is now a commitment to make this standard practice. Such guidance probably needs to be produced institution by institution, depending on the terms of TEL support available. Ideally, attention to accessibility would be explicitly included as part of the marking criteria for digital content, so that it becomes standard to flag up accessibility issues (such as we already bring attention to plagiarism). Once set in place, with guidance provided by IT staff, this should not be onerous for teachers to bring attention to. Moving towards new assessment types is to be welcomed in terms of reinvigorating traditional disciplines, but it also requires training students in accessibility, above and beyond producing accessible teaching materials.

Engaging with Disability Discrimination Law

Anti-discrimination law is not often referenced when considering EDI issues in Classics. There is value to engaging with this legislation, not least because it deals with the lived experiences and situations of certain groups who are prone to be discriminated against, and it therefore faces the complexities and conflicts between individuals head-on. In addition to being practical, it needs to be rather philosophical in nature—what is 'fairness' or 'equality'?

'Disability' is an umbrella term that covers impairments, conditions, and chronic illnesses that can have very little in common with each other. A deaf person has no particular insight into what it means to use a wheelchair, and the strains of undergoing treatment for cancer is a very different experience from how a blind or partially sighted person navigates the world. Furthermore, individuals within each group will have their own response to their situation. One link that does unite most if not all those with a significant, life-changing disability is the impact on time. Your disability may cost money, or it may not, but it is difficult to think of a disability that does not consume time, in some cases greedily vacuuming it up so that difficult life choices need to be made. Similarly, it is highly likely—or inevitable—that those providing reasonable adjustments may find it difficult to find the time and attention to deal with the situation. But find it they must. Anti-discrimination law for disabled people bears more of a duty for individuals and institutions than most other protected characteristics, namely in the requirement to provide 'reasonable adjustments.'

I have organised a training session for LAHP (London Arts and Humanities Partnership) PhD students to consider the implications of the 2010 Equality Act. This session thought about how knowledge of Human Rights law might enhance research into particular characteristics, and what bearing disability rights issues might have on traditional research questions. One example given was rethinking 'the viewer' in antiquity bearing in mind different types of visual impairment, another was the relationship between audio description and ekphrasis, and how we communicate about visual/material culture. The afternoon was spent in the British Museum, as an Access All Senses event (see below). What distinguished this training session was thinking not only about the legal/moral reasons for making research accessible, but also the intellectual benefits of doing so.

I have also organised a departmental away day for KCL Classics staff led by Robert Wintemute, Professor of Human Rights Law at Kings. While this legislation is far too much to consider in a morning, there is room to explore the history of anti-discrimination law and how and why it stands as it does now, and then in turn to apply this to research questions that touch upon the relevant identities, statuses, and characteristics. The morning was divided into:

- Introduction to the 2010 Equality Act
- Focus on disability and reasonable adjustments
- When the interests of different protected characteristics clash, focusing on *Lee v Ashers Baking Co Ltd* (the 'support gay marriage' cake case)
- the difference between positive action (lawful) and positive discrimination (unlawful).

Thinking about the history of anti-discrimination law is a reminder that human rights are not 'natural' as such, but artificially constructed and come into law over time.[4] Before 1965, there was no anti-discrimination law at all in the UK. Even today, there is no guarantee that individuals will experience the benefits of this protection, as it depends on a comprehensive public awareness of what these duties are, and access to legal aid to enforce them. At times, implementing such rights is less than straightforward—particularly when different rights seem to contradict each other. The 2010 Equality Act could be seen as a blueprint for good citizen conduct, applying to everyone (including those who have been historically marginalised or disadvantaged themselves). It can be weaponised to fight against discrimination, but it is mainly designed as a code of behaviour to prevent legal action from being necessary. Bringing separate laws into one Act (as occurred with the passing of the 2010 Equality Act) equalises the seriousness of various types of discrimination (for example, it does not allow for some rights to be considered 'more equal' or important than others).

This disability discrimination law hangs on the deliberately vague term, 'reasonable adjustment.' Passed in 1995, the Disability Discrimination Act offered a crucial change in policy: disabled people's impairment or condition was no longer 'just their problem,' but there was a shared duty for all to overcome the barriers that these individuals encountered in public life. However, the law does not promise a magic wand for people with disabilities, and the accommodations required must be 'reasonable.' This law marks a shift from the charity model, whereby society and individuals might help disabled people as benevolent aid in exchange for gratitude, to disability rights as human rights, with the expectation of getting the support as a standard. This progress was hard won, following the 'Capital Crawl' protest in America and comparable direct action in Britain (see, for example, the British film 'Then Barbara met Alan' for a dramatisation of this movement).

There are many good reasons for having a sound awareness of this kind of legislation, beyond citizen duties. In addition to providing accessibility for students, removing the stigma of disability (partly so that disabled staff are welcomed, and those with less visible disabilities stop masking and become role models), and training students to produce accessible materials in their later careers, I argue that increased disability awareness can enhance and enlighten research projects.

In Britain, the 1995 Disability Discrimination Act imposed the duty on public bodies, such as museums, to make their venues accessible. As well as producing visible changes, such as disabled toilets and ramps, this led to the thriving scene of audio description (AD) and touch tours for blind and partially sighted people, and British Sign Language (BSL) tours for Deaf people. When using museums as a classroom and considering their access programmes, we see that there are also many positive payoffs from thinking about antiquity through a disability lens.

'Access All Senses': Exploring Accessibility in the Parthenon Galleries

Since 2018, I have led a project with museum access staff, under the name 'Museum Access Network for Sensory Impairments, London' or MANSIL (www.mansil.uk). This involved exploring the access programmes in numerous London museums for blind and partially sighted people (mainly AD and touch tours) and Deaf-led BSL tours. Through a close engagement with access activities, the project seeks to shed light on a number of research questions. For example, AD is a form of intermodal translation, from the visual or sensory appreciation of art and material culture to the vivid, almost poetic verbal English. How does this process enable us to engage more deeply with visual culture? What role does and can touch have in art appreciation? And does a visual-spatial sign language communicate more directly with visual-material culture than linear, spoken English?

On one level, therefore, this project invites academics to explore the intellectual value of access programmes, which has traditionally been neglected. This is possibly because activities related to disabled people were considered insubstantial and had nothing to teach researchers. Or it may simply be the ableism that 'forgets' people with sensory impairments. For example, in the field of sensory studies, 'the viewer' is generally assumed to have 20:20 vision—but people experience sight in a variety of ways.

This project considers some of the insights that these conditions can have. In activist terms, this is called 'Deaf Gain' or 'Blind Gain.' For example, having limited sight can result in paying more attention to what you are looking at. Some conditions, like stereoscopy or colour blindness, mean that the person literally sees the world differently. Deaf people are a linguistic minority if their preferred language is BSL. What is less explored is how this visual-spatial language might provide a shortcut to engaging with visual-material culture—the visual, performative nature of sign languages has certain advantages over the more limited mode of speech.

I have organised 'Access All Senses' events to introduce these three forms of communication to mainstream, sighted and hearing people (see downloadable booklets designed for pop-ups in the Courtauld Gallery and the British Museum: www.mansil.uk/museum-pop-ups). We will focus on the latter here, which is home to the Tiresias project. This project, named after the blind seer of Greek myth, culminated in 1998 with the opening of auxiliary Rooms 18a and 18b and the publication of *Second Sight of the Parthenon Frieze* (Bird et al. 1998).

The Parthenon marbles are world-famous, not least for their controversial acquisition, and Greece's demands for their return. That debate aside, the British Museum Parthenon collection is notable as one of the side auxiliary rooms was designed for blind and partially sighted people. Opened in 1998, in response to the 1995 Disability Discrimination Act, Room 18b was designed for touch, with Braille and raised line drawings available throughout. There is a touch model of the Parthenon, and casts of the casts from the West Frieze can be touched. This space is also to be used by sighted people—so it is integrationist. It was cutting edge, and based on contemporary understanding of what blind people needed. Reopening just before Covid shut museums in 2020, it has been re-designed, as feedback indicated that sighted people had made assumptions that were not quite what was required. For example, raised line drawings provided without further audio or in-person support are not as helpful as had been assumed: fingertips cannot replace sight in this way. It was also impossible for blind visitors to know that Braille lay under the English text to be felt, as there was no notice to this effect. This Braille, with the raised line drawings, has been removed, although a guide was planned to provide this if required. The space is also now far better lit. Several AD clips are also available on Soundcloud, again useful for both sighted and blind people.

In the Access All Senses events, BSL was introduced to hearing visitors with a Deaf tour leader and BSL interpreter to facilitate communication. They were able to showcase elements of BSL grammar, beyond the perhaps obvious element of iconicity and mime. For example, role shift is when the signer becomes various different characters, people, animals or even inanimate objects in a story, signalling the shifts through body language and eye gaze. BSL allows for zooming and changing perspectives. Spatial verbs indicate the direction of action (e.g., the 'I ask you' sign moves from the signer to the other person, while 'you ask me' the opposite way). The space in front of the signer is the canvas, and this suits the spatial element of art.

So, what did the visitors make of this? It was a self-selecting group (people not interested in this would simply walk pass). But the feedback forms collected were very positive: people liked the embodiment of BSL, it made them feel more connected with the art, making it more memorable, and just overall more engaging. This event was able to promote BSL and the idea that Deaf people could lead tours (and not just be 'cared for' with access provided to them). But it was also able to open up explorations into how a visual-spatial language can be used to communicate visual-spatial art.

This approach also gave the opportunity to consider the role of touch in art appreciation—even though touch is not normally allowed in museums. However, blind and partially sighted people are often allowed to touch objects that sighted people are not. Is this an element of art appreciation that most of us have forgotten and been excluded from? Touch is used to help substitute the museum experience sighted people have, although it cannot replace sight, and it is popular among this community.

Another aim was to consider the development of touch description. AD is the vivid, verbal description of visual culture (Fryer 2016). Can we do the same kind of intermodal translation for tactile culture? This seems to be much more challenging. However, some blind people have pointed out that, as they have access to handle objects, they could provide access through their testimony in return. This does open up the wider question about how little touch description there is in art history. Touch is a transgression in the museum context, which may partly explain our current poverty of language regarding it—beyond binary adjectives, such as hard/soft, we are much less practiced and polished in the description of tactile experience.

I have also wanted to explore using AD in the classroom, partly to explore how sighted people engage with it (see also Adams 2021). Snyder (2008, 194) argues that 'using AD techniques for the description of static images and exhibitions not only enhances accessibility, but it also helps develop more expressive, vivid, and imaginative museum tours.' AD can guide sighted people, help them engage with artworks, and increase memorability (Eardley et al. 2017, 195). Cachia (2017, in a paper in *Art Journal*) suggests that AD might become part of visual studies. In one class, I showed Alma-Tadema's 'Phidias Showing the Frieze of the Parthenon to his Friends' (1868) to students for a short period of time (28.63 seconds; this is the mean average people look at a painting (and label) in art galleries: Smith et al. 2017). After the slide was switched off, they drew or described the painting. They then listened to an AD while viewing the painting again, to begin to see what had been missed—even by those who knew the painting before. The use of AD was welcomed and not seen as too basic or a waste of time.

Marking criteria often encourages or demands an explicit 'analytical' approach from students, while descriptive writing is considered the much poorer cousin. Interpretation and argument are indeed a key skillset developed in the Arts and Humanities, but the skill of a rich description is one to be acknowledged and rewarded as well. We tend to encourage students to write about what an object or image can mean or indicate, but not so much to use words and space to *describe*. The poetic intermodal translation from the visual/sensory to the vivid verbal is not just a difficult and accomplished achievement, but it is also a transferable skill, to all areas of marketing or copywriting, for example. Given the attention to ekphrasis in Classics, it is highly appropriate to take time and attention to training students in doing this themselves.

AD can also be used as a fun ice-breaker. Ask a student to provide an AD of an image that their peer or group cannot see (it works in couples or larger audiences), who are asked to draw what they believe is being described. The results can be very varied, but it's a good game! It also encourages students to state the obvious in their descriptions, which for various reasons (looking stupid, not being *analytical* enough), can be very difficult to get them to do. As drawing an object makes the viewer look much more closely, so does describing it.

Conclusion; Action Beyond Access

'Nothing about us, without us' is the disability rights mantra—don't think you know what's best for us! As we have seen, the Tiresias project in the British Museum has changed in response to users' feedback—the original curators were sighted, while working on current knowledge and advice from charities. The target audience, in this case, blind and partially sighted people, must remain in the forefront when designing these spaces. With this in mind, this project then considers whether these provisions and approaches can then be applied to the mainstream experience. Likewise, the open presence of disabled teachers in HE will serve not only as role models, but also as a reminder that students themselves will need to work in accessible ways in the wider world.

The MANSIL project bridges academia and museum access work— and the Tiresias project was originally prompted by the new DDA of 1995. We therefore see a triangle of law, academia, and cultural institutions. While I have led this research project, it relies on listening to others' experiences and expertise, rather than *imagining* what these experiences are like. It is innovative because ableist views of art appreciation are not assumed. The museum not only takes the position of informing or educating the visitors, but also transforms into a platform for creative exchange, whereby all learn and benefit. The strategies that have been developed by and for people with sensory impairments, such as AD, can benefit a wider demographic, leaving inclusive education good for all.

Notes

1. See also Morris (2021) on use of American terminology.
2. Leonard and Lovatt (2020).
3. Government Accessibility Guidance, https://www.gov.uk/service-manual/helping-people-to-use-your-service/making-your-service-accessible-an-introduction#meeting-government-accessibility-requirements (accessed 3 April 2022).
4. Hepple (2014).

Works Cited

Adams, E. (2021) 'New Light on "the Viewer": Sensing the Parthenon Galleries in the British Museum', in E. Adams (ed.), *Disability Studies and the Classical Body*, Abingdon, 130–60.

Bird, S., Jenkins, I. and Levi, F. (1998) *Second Sight of the Parthenon Frieze*, Turin.

Cachia, A. (2017) 'Curating New Openings: Rethinking Diversity in the Gallery', *Art Journal* 76.3–4: 48–50.

Eardley, A., Fryer, L., Hutchinson, R., Cock, M., Ride, P. and Neves, J. (2017) 'Enriched Audio Description: Working Towards an Inclusive Museum Experience', in S. Halder and L. Czop Assaf (eds.), *Inclusion, Disability and Culture*, Cham, 195–207.

Fryer, L. (2016) *An Introduction to Audio Description*, Abingdon.

Hepple, B. (2014) *Equality: The Legal Framework*, vol. 2, London.

Leonard, V. and Lovatt, H. (2020) 'Council of University Classical Departments Equality and Diversity Report 2020', *CUCD EDI Blog*, 1–76.

Morris, A. (2021) 'A Brief Guide to Disability Terminology and Theory in Ancient World Studies', *SCS Blog*, https://classicalstudies.org/scs-blog/alexandra-morris/blog-brief-guide-disability-terminology-and-theory-ancient-world-studies (accessed 15 April 2022).

Smith, L., Smith, J. and Tinio, P. (2017) 'Time Spent Viewing Art and Reading Labels', *Psychology of Aesthetics, Creativity and the Arts* 11: 77–85.

Snyder, J. (2008) 'Audio Description: the Visual Made Verbal', in J. Díaz-Cintas (ed.), *The Didactics of Audiovisual Translation*, Amsterdam, 191–8.

9 'Reaching Out with Eurydice'
The Myth and Voice Initiative

Efrossini Spentzou

Introduction

Students and a member of staff (Efi Spentzou) at the Department of Classics and the School of Humanities of Royal Holloway, University of London, have embarked on a public engagement project called The Myth and Voice Initiative. The project aims to provide safe spaces for engagement with feelings, emotions, obstacles, and solutions surrounding the use of voice and personal expression encouraging story telling for community building. The initial focus is on secondary school children. As we gain expertise and gather experience, the aspiration is to scope and engage with potential partners beyond the classroom such as youth foundations, community centres, and shelters in the hope that the initiative, with the involvement of appropriate and qualified collaborators, can play a role in programs of self-development, social inclusion, and mental well-being.

In its current phase, the project works through a series of experiential workshops based on selected characters and story lines from Ovid's *Metamorphoses*. These provide a safe 'othered' environment in which young people can grapple with contemporary dilemmas and challenges. The mythological setting creates an emotional distance. Similar cover is afforded by the role-play elements in the reimagining of the ancient stories. Such distancing features create a safe space away from the everyday experience in which the young participants can explore voices and suppressions and develop an empathetic approach to the unfamiliar. The mythological context provides a neutral narrative space which is abstracted from contemporary cultural values allowing participants from varying cultural backgrounds to engage creatively and personally with the potential of the mythic narrative.

The workshops were initially developed as in-class delivery, but have been adapted for online provision as well. There is a growing

DOI: 10.4324/9781003278016-10

roster of workshops working with different myths and focusing on different issues. The first workshop centres on the myth of Eurydice and Orpheus as a story of muted self-expression and the strains behind young love. A further workshop is based on Arachne and plays out the contemporary reception (in social media and elsewhere) of a powerful (female) voice. Another engages with the myth of Phaethon and invites participants to reflect on issues and consequences around difficult father/son relationships and teenage angst. A fourth one engages with Io and explores issues around forced mobility, homelessness, and their relation to abuse. The last one currently in the pipeline uses the myth of Persephone to engage with gendered and generational conflict within relationships (and marriages).

This initiative is a richly layered collaboration that tests conventional hierarchies of pedagogy. The materials are co-created with different cohorts of our university students as a scaffold to frame the creativity and provide the space for the voices of the school students to emerge. Their voices are at the heart of the project and they inform our experiences and the various iterations of the workshops. The university students volunteer in the co-creation of materials; offer their insights and perspectives and, in turn, learn as they teach and later as they themselves prepare to facilitate in workshops in their former school communities. My role in this adventure continually shifts. I propose the projects and develop an initial framework, but then each workshop has tipping points of role reversal. I am always aware of the need to inspire trust and curiosity in support of the students' creativity. I simultaneously witness the students educating me as to what it feels like 'to see themselves' in the myths. I elicit responses and I am learning to resist the teacher's inclination, acquired from years of occupying the 'leading' seat in the classroom, to smoothen out or 'polish' their thoughts and the materials we are putting together. 'Rawness' can be a virtue.[1]

Similarly, working with the school communities, I am learning the fine balance which makes these events special. They are normally offered as 'enrichment events'; an opportunity for the pupils to move beyond their familiar experiences, to engage with new forms of learning, and be motivated to think 'outside the box'. The workshops offer the students opportunities to adopt different voices and roles to those normally available to them in curricular classroom work. Crucially, these are experiential offerings hoping to grow student confidence and generate self-belief through safely engaging with unfamiliar narratives. Such engagements link the (often alien) Classical world to the students' own life experiences. They legitimate their responses to those narratives, provide access to and ownership of Classical traditions, and valorise their own life-worlds, experiences, and voices in the conjunction of narratives. Classical mythology is the kind of cultural capital for which many participants seem to feel the need for permission to access, but the workshops aspire to provide creative freedom that empowers the students to bring the myths to their home ground. That ownership of the story, generated in the permission to rework and re-voice it, creates a meaningful relationship so that hierarchical knowledge takes a back seat as they try out different placements of themselves into the debates sparked by the myth.[2]

Everyone involved in this engaged pedagogy[3] has been growing. In this short article, I reflect on the early experiences of co-creating the first workshops and the first school visits. This reflective account incorporates diverse voices and feedback from several groups in an attempt to explore the impact of the virtual or real flipped classroom experiences on the different constituencies involved. It also explores new perspectives on the dynamics of power underpinning Classical myth and indeed Classics, in general, which emerge through these engagements.

I am grateful to our inspiring co-creator students at Royal Holloway who have given time and energy generously, to the schools that have already put their trust in the Initiative and, last but not least, to the editors of the present volume for making space for a first critical evaluation of the initiative as it gathers momentum and expands.

Designing the First Workshop

A few years ago, I embarked on a research project on twentieth- and twenty-first-century rewritings of Eurydice. For that project, I looked into poetry, theatre, film, musical art, and a graphic novel. These stories feature Eurydices as a 17-year-old Sixth Former in Northumbria, an American middle-aged woman starting again after divorce, a boy in love with another boy spending the night in a Parisian hospital, an Indian popular singer moving to America to seek fame, an unemployed girl in the American South during the 1930s Depression Era, and various others.[4] The diversity and innovation are striking: time and again artists return to Eurydice and in many instances are haunted by her relative silence. Some allow her to speak, daring her to rebellious thoughts or to explore the multiple forms of silencing in our contemporary world.

At the same time, in our final year UG module Contemporary Approaches to Latin Literature student contributions often revolved

around issues of gendered behaviours, voices, ventriloquisms, and (un)safe spaces in male-authored texts and my adventures with modern Eurydices made it into the conversation. Why was Eurydice useful to these modern artists? What did Eurydice allow them to talk about? When I asked the students what most bothered them about Eurydice and her silence they came up with:
How did Eurydice feel about:

a   Orpheus?
b   being robbed of her second chance?
c   being only remembered as part of his story?
d   her life in the underworld?
e   her life lost in the world above?

It was at this point that we decided to take the myth out of class and workshop it. The group saw it as an opportunity for Classical reception in action and to insert their personality and interests into the myth. But more, it became an invitation to explore their own thinking about themselves not in a confessional context but in empathy with a silent stranger, another person needing help, support, understanding, and friendship. Rather than constraining expression, the myth provided a safe space for creative exploration and it very quickly became obvious that the exercise had potentially beneficial effects far beyond an improvement of the students' understanding of Latin literature.

What followed was the creation of a 'Eurydice group,' tasked to put together an experiential workshop using Eurydice as the silent woman 'next door.' Conversations addressed lived or narrated experiences of marginalisation, of friends struggling to get heard, understood, and validated. The axes of marginalisation expanded from gender to encompass race, sexuality, and class. The need to address silence and being silenced as marginalisation was evident and not much of a surprise to anyone familiar with race and gender issues. As the conversation progressed, attention also turned to silence as a choice to be respected and understood. It was clear that the group was exercised by the silent figure metaphorically standing in front of them. They experienced (again?) the block that is often felt when someone we encounter withholds their speech. We became more alert to the dangers of appropriating Eurydice's silence.

The discussions opened up problems: how do we respect silence? How do we provide space and safety for the silenced ones? What happens when we put ourselves 'in someone else's shoes?' How can we be sensitive to those shoes belonging to someone else, potentially of a different culture, outlook, and experiences? The mythic narrative provided not just narrative forms but also scope for nuance.

The putting together of the workshop brought together the students' interests. One student (who went on to study stage management) developed ideas of hot-seating and devised short theatrical activities for role-playing. Another student wrote a short poem for Eurydice modelling a response for participants. Another created a sensitive summary of the original story (from Ovid's *Metamorphoses*). We all shaped and re-shaped the talking points, gauging age-appropriateness, acknowledging potential limitations in delivery, and visualising pathways to participation.

As we shifted from student café to online during the first Covid lockdown in the Spring and Summer of 2020, the students displayed enthusiasm, energy, freshness of ideas, and above all deep empathy. They could relate to the school-age students and imagine ways to welcome the diversity of potential participants, attitudes, personalities, and educational preferences. They highlighted the key issues that they imagined would intrigue the participants. In designing a workshop on speaking and listening, they became conscious of their silent colleagues, drawing them in and harnessing their thoughts and attitudes in the service of future participants.

It was a deeply satisfying experience of reaching across and connecting and putting together the workshop. In the summer of 2020, it also worked, one might say, as group therapy in a traumatic time for everyone involved. But only practice would tell whether this experiment was going to work outside the university.

School Visits

At the point of writing this, the workshop has had three outings so far, all after school hours: a purely online experience with one of the original student co-creators as a facilitator, a virtual visit from me to a school with the students in class, and a face-to-face event with two Y13 students of the same school as facilitators in the class. In all three occasions, we had between 20 and 30 participants. Each event was special and a bit different, as circumstances of delivery also differed. One event was open to students from across Years 8–11 (i.e., addressing 12- to 15-year-old pupils), the other was addressed to the Sixth Form (16–18-year-olds) and the third to a Year 10 cohort (14–15-year-olds). Thanks are due to Miss Jessica Angel, Head of History at Cambourne Village College, Cambridgeshire, Ms Morgan Williams of the Harris Federation, London, and Dr Thalia Sini-Spencer, Head of Classics at Bishop Thomas Grant School, Lambeth, London for providing a smooth experience before and during the sessions and supporting their students throughout.

a) Virtually: Class in School; Facilitator Virtual (October 2021)

The class was comprised of a number of small groups of friends who came and sat and worked together for the activities. Younger and older tried their hand with the talking points. Curiosity about silent Eurydice emerged as the students began to appreciate the gaps in her story (what we don't find in the text about her). Together, we created scenarios as to her short life and experiences before her untimely death. The younger children tended to elaborate on the everyday experiences of this elusive figure: how had she lived? The older students were more exercised by those elements in her life that may have engendered silence: they spent a significant part of their talking time trying to imagine Eurydice's upbringing. It was clear that the cultural distance of this ancient tale encouraged a few of them to wonder, and others to attempt to explain, what it might mean to be growing up and experiencing early romantic relationships in a variety of modern cultures, so not just drawing from their own immediate experiences.

Eurydice mattered for that group. They saw her as if she were a friend from a family they did not fully understand. Her elusiveness worried them. Her difference did not lead to her categorisation as 'other' and thus beyond what 'we' should worry about. The evident cultural and experiential differences were not seen as insuperable obstacles to understanding. Ultimately, the narrative worked as a reminder of silences encountered today and of an experience of difference. One comment collected in a final reflection put it succinctly: *'I feel quite strongly about people being given a voice, and this unfairness [in Eurydice's story] is something we should really learn from and use while we're living in the now.'*

The experience left me acutely aware of the participants' willingness and desire to respond to a call for 'listening to the other.' Despite the challenges inherent in a virtual visit to a full classroom, many of them stood up and used their voice to respond to an unfamiliar event and to fill in for Eurydice's silence. They adopted a variety of interpretative angles, and in the process became increasingly aware of the variety of narrative possibilities behind Eurydice's silence. They felt the dangers of misconceptions and misunderstanding.

The students came to this unusual event in friendship groups but the opportunity for individual reaction meant that responses did not 'flatten out' or become consensus-driven. Those who worked alone often produced contributions which came across as particularly empathetic. It thus seemed to me that the workshop met diverse needs. Some participants were likely drawn to the experiential workshop by an urge to experiment with the unfamiliar and play out roles in the company of friends. Others were moved to explore stories of reticence and to think through issues of cultural difference. The workshop needed to provide for diversity of interaction and had the responsibility to cater for, and support, diverse needs and ambitions.

b) Online: All Participants Online from Home (March 2021)

The online-only event was open to 16–18-year-olds and the virtual space proved most conducive to a more personal engagement as all participants responded primarily as individuals. The medium and circumstances created unique challenges. These were managed by having two facilitators, myself and a university student co-facilitator, and we variously used breakout rooms to work in more intimate groups. Yet, the online delivery also brought advantages: it allowed a less socially policed space that empowered expression. I never saw the faces or heard the voices of the participants, but the communication via chat was imaginative, uninhibited, and expressive. It offered invaluable opportunities to engage with the different ways these young people respond to silence. There was no temptation to reach for the safety of group think here and I could tell that some contributions were using Eurydice's silence as an invitation to articulate their own understanding and experience of difficult relationships.

There was a greater inclination in this group of older teenagers to interpret Eurydice's silence as a manifestation of an awkward relationship with Orpheus and that untreated aspect of the story featured prominently in the discussion. Orpheus' fame and musical talent were seen as an off-putting and distancing quality. Before long there was talk in the chat about arranged marriages and similar culture-specific explorations of marital and romantic relationships. One particularly articulate comment followed up by imagining Eurydice's societal and familiar background. The implication, there, as I understood it, was that her silence might have been a defensive tactic and an acquired mode of existence born out of expectations from her upbringing. The contributions of this group struck me as a fascinating blend of curiosity, awareness, observation, and experience. I was also intensely aware of the delicate dynamics and self-conscious nature of the exchange: our locational dispersion was a major obstacle in any attempt to create a community, discouraging communication; and yet, the chat was successful in eliciting communication from those more reticent participants who might have remained silent in a classroom environment, reluctant to experience the exposure of an oral contribution. The chat function provided a space in which people could not be talked over and in which comments could be weighed carefully. 'Silence spoke' and the multiple modes of silencing a woman provoked the group's reflection.

c) In Class: Students and Facilitators in the Same Room (December 2021)

Being all together in this traditional mode of delivery of the event generated a palpable sense of a co-creating and creative community. This workshop had a great sense of dynamism and of breaking the boundaries between deliverers and receivers. Participants gradually embraced their capacity to change the ancient story by listening to and working with one another's suggestions and ideas. A special space of belonging was felt to be emerging as the discussions became more confident, and the students, sitting in circles, started filling in the empty spaces in the narrative, participating in the story by tuning in to elements that spoke most vividly to them.[5] Some of the students in this workshop had prior knowledge of the Classical world through formal study so they had to un-think the critical methodologies they already had and respond to the story in an unaccustomed way. They were aware that the story belonged to a distant and somewhat privileged site of knowledge, often held in awe and distanced from the here and now, sheltered behind a 'dead' language owned by a small minority. By asking them to unpick and alter this story, the workshop provided encouragement for them to reconstruct playfully their relationship with the past, and with Classics and its traditions, and reframe it as something more intimate and domestic, speaking to their own concerns. As with the others, they also came to 'own' the story in a new way.

As the narrative possibilities were filled out and the story opened up to imaginative reinventions, the collapse of communication and trust between the couple seemed to be one of the starkest messages. This for many was of personal value and a trigger for reflection; as one final reflection put it: '*I learned that when you are in a relationship with someone, it is important for it to be genuine or some people will get hurt.*' This group was swift to imagine the underworld as a place where Eurydice could be free to be herself (and they had not read Carol Ann Duffy's Eurydice)[6].

The group was now able to see through the charm of the famous singer and his story: '*I learnt that the main character doesn't always have to be the most interesting*' read one short comment. By the end, Eurydice, the young woman from the distant past was a friend they could joke with: '*don't get married*' wrote one and '*do not go near snakes*' added another before drawing more serious 'life' lessons from the experience.

Moving Forwards, Seeking New Partners

Further workshops are being planned with new cohorts of our university students. A group of first- and second-year students have tested out the Eurydice workshop and offered tweaks on the format. We then designed together the Arachne workshop. The myth produced animated discussion on modern forms of authoritative power as the group used the ancient fearless girl to evoke numerous grass-root political movements that mattered to them, such as Black Lives Matter, youth movements seeking to expose big corporations working against local communities, or companies investing in fossil fuel. Even the fan-based protest against the prospect of a European Super League got a mention as a successful example of speaking through to power.

In their evaluation, the students expressed satisfaction at the invitation they had to think with the story 'as themselves' and in the collective effort to see themselves into this myth. As one of them put it: '*Often when I read myths, I think about their relation to modern oppression and power dynamics, but I sometimes feel a bit awkward bringing up those conversations as a student of colour. I'm happy that I've been able to have these important discussions with fellow students, and I'm grateful for opportunities to listen to and learn from my peers.*'

The next step takes the Initiative out of the Classics department and into Drama, to co-create a workshop on Phaethon. The students involved have recently finished 'Telling Tales', a third-year module exploring storytelling practices that utilise myth, folklore, and oral history to engage with present-day issues. Drawing from their recent experiences in group dynamics, role-play, and other similar improvisational techniques, the students will draw from Phaethon's myth to narrate difficult father-son relationships and, depending also on how the story will resonate with them, the delicate relationship between humans and the environment. They will then put together the workshop to be offered to schools and other settings. As well as empowering the students to 'find a voice' for themselves and for difficult experiences, the workshop is designed as a professional development tool for those wishing to explore mentoring roles in the future.

The co-creating and mentoring intricately embedded and blended into the initiative have been amongst its most fulfilling elements so far. Working with Classical myth and storytelling, the various groups of participants are mentored, while also they become co-creators and mentors in a dynamic process enabling self-expression, self-discovery, and personal growth. In my next school visit, the hosting teacher has asked to embed this interdependence and skills more centrally in our collaboration: we will run the workshop for a small group of year 10s, discuss their experience as participants, and support them to become facilitators in running the workshop at a later day for the whole Year 8 cohort in their school, subsequently discussing their self-assessment and evaluation of the latter event.

The whole initiative is an exercise in inclusive Classical reception, exploring how ancient mythic narratives provide structures through which we can explore cultural experiences. With its emphasis on social equity, co-creation, and storytelling as a means of (re)discovering one's self, the initiative has the ambition to showcase a novel position and role for the Classics in contemporary programs of community building, self-development and discovery, active citizenship. In due course, it aspires to develop partnerships with educational centres in the community, mental health charities, young carers' trusts, and a variety of similar settings. Building confidence and expertise in communicating with vulnerable people is one of my own needs in bringing this project forward beyond more conventional educational settings. I also look forward to acquiring new partners, at all levels, to continue this journey together.

Notes

1 For a thoughtful account of the value of the ephemeral, mindful, and personal in experiential community-building workshops of this type, see Wardrop et al. (2020).
2 Despite the stark difference of settings involved, Dib and Faccani (2021) have offered me an illuminating reflection of opportunities and challenges in such an experiential and ad hoc mode of teaching, built on their experience of teaching Ovid to incarcerated students.
3 My work and this project draws inspiration from insights and critical reflection on the classroom as participatory and self-actualising space offered by bel hooks (1994), esp. 13–22.
4 Cf. Spentzou (2018) for a first taste.
5 For more on the intricate dynamics of such 'potential spaces' in the related field of drama therapy see Pearson (2013).
6 Duffy (1999, 58–62).

Works Cited

Dib, N. and Faccani, O. (2021) 'Teaching Ovid to Incarcerated Students: An Experiential Analysis', in E. Capettini and N.S. Rabinowitz (eds.), *Classics and Prison Education in the US*, Abingdon, 77–86.
Duffy, C.A. (1999) *The World's Wife*, London.
hooks, b. (1994) *Teaching to Transgress: Education as the Practice of Freedom*, London.
Pearson, J. (2013) 'Entering the World of Stories', in J. Pearson, M. Smail and P. Watts (eds.), *Dramatherapy With Myth and Fairytale*, London, 41–54.
Spentzou, E. (2018) 'Many Un/happy Returns from Eurydice', in S. Frangoulidis and S. Harrison (eds.), *Life, Love, and Death in Latin Poetry*, Berlin, 295–311.
Wardrop, A., Huntley, G. and Kilgallon, S. (2020) 'Transforming Knowledge: Using Arts-Based Activity to Explore Classics and Therapeutic Practice', in J. Laewers, H. Schwall and J. Opsomer (eds.), *Psychology and the Classics*, Berlin, 109–26.

10 Inclusive Classics and Pedagogy
Teachers, Academics, and Students in Conversation

Barbara Goff and Alexia Petsalis-Diomidis

This chapter reflects the opening panel of the 2021 Classical Association annual conference which took place online.[1] We were invited to organise a panel because of our Inclusive Classics Initiative launched in 2020 which offers an inclusive platform for conversations—sometimes difficult ones—that aim to help shape our discipline in a more equitable and liberatory mould.[2] A key feature of this initiative and its events is to enact inclusivity by actively seeking out voices which have been, and still are, marginalised and by eschewing polarising discourses. The exchange of ideas amongst academics at a variety of levels and their students, as well as school teachers and pupils, has been an important feature from the outset. The use of online events is a way of reaching diverse and international audiences, while we have continually experimented with formats.[3] The Inclusive Classics Initiative foregrounds successful modes of making classics increasingly inclusive, thus amplifying positive work and voices which might otherwise not be heard. At the same time, it recognises that there is yet much work to be done for the discipline to become truly inclusive, in its demographic makeup and in the objects of scrutiny and its epistemic modes.

The 2021 CA panel, and this chapter, are purposely multivocal: they include the perspectives of both learners and teachers from the university and school sectors. Contributors were asked to consider the question 'In your experience in what ways is classics suited to inclusive teaching and learning?'. The most important themes which arise in these reflections are recognising diversity in the ancient world and its receptions and in working to centre that diversity. Responding to the varied needs of learners, particularly the desire to see themselves reflected in the objects of study, emerges in a number of pieces. The contributions demonstrate in miniature form the critical reassessment that our discipline is undergoing. We highlight two elements crucial to the process of reflecting on how we want to shape our

DOI: 10.4324/9781003278016-11

discipline: putting aside the fantasy of classical exceptionalism and foregrounding classical reception studies in order to confront and analyse the multifarious responses to classics in and beyond academia.

Tim Whitmarsh, A. G. Leventis Professor of Greek Culture, University of Cambridge

John Pentland Mahaffy wrote in the introduction to *Social Life in Ancient Greece* (1874) that 'if one of us were transported to Periclean Athens, provided he were a man of high culture, he would find life and manners strangely like our own' (p. 3). Mahaffy wrote as an Anglo-Irish apologist for the British Empire, and there is little doubt to whom Mahaffy's 'us' refers. This kind of gesture is very familiar: 'men of high culture' have often identified closely with aspects of the Greco-Roman world. Mahaffy's pact of complicity is, in fact, doubly exclusive: not only does he marginalise those in the modern world who are not men or 'of high culture,' but also he explicitly (a little beforehand) declares that other ancient societies, such as the Egyptians and 'Hebrews,' would find the modern western world utterly alien.

The position Mahaffy adopted was neither neutral nor self-evident. He set himself firmly against those historians who would 'reduce the motives of society to rude violence and successful force' (p. 5). He wrote at a time when new models were emerging that questioned the idea that Greco-Roman culture was founded on civilised rationality. These ideas would in due course issue into the anthropologically influenced scholarship loosely identified with the 'Cambridge Ritualists,' who emphasised the strange otherness of the ancient world, deliberately challenging the idea that Greeks and Romans were 'proto-Europeans' (let alone proto-Christians). This ethnographic focus on the 'otherness' of Greeks and Romans has often carried with it a political charge. Nicole Loraux and Jean-Pierre Vernant, the late twentieth century's primary champions of 'anthropological' Classics, were intellectually shaped by the climate of post-war left-wing anti-fascism.

In the early twenty-first century, we are still to an extent locked into this debate. How like 'us' the Greeks and the Romans were remains a live issue in scholarship, blogs and wider culture, and on social media. In its modern form, this discourse typically manifests itself either as a crypto-Mahaffian celebration of the Greeks and the Romans as the originators of western civilisation, or as a pugnacious assault on them as embodiments of values that all right-minded people should reject. Both approaches, however, are reductive and simplistic and rest upon an implicit assumption that both 'we,' modern observers, and 'them,'

Inclusive Classics and Pedagogy 123

the ancients we contemplate, are single groups unified by shared values. One positive thing we have learned in our fragmented age is that societies (all of them) are extraordinarily diverse. It is time to kick our addiction to looking to classical antiquity for grand paradigms of moral behaviour, whether positive or negative, and acknowledge instead that diversity and social complexity are the very stuff of history.

Tristan Craig, Undergraduate in 'Ancient and Medieval History,' University of Edinburgh

As a then 26-year-old, entering Higher Education after a gap of some five years, my route into undergraduate study was quite unlike that of most of my peers. Not only did I have a significant hiatus in my education, but my introduction to Classics had consisted of just a few weeks studying Herodotus, Suetonius, and Ovid during a year-long Access Programme. Despite my anxieties about entering a field in which I had very little background knowledge, I was pleasantly surprised to find that there was no presumption that I would have undertaken any Classical Studies before entering university. Language arguably presents one of the biggest barriers to studying Classics at undergraduate level; however, I do not feel at all disadvantaged by choosing a non-language-based Ancient and Medieval History degree. Rather, it has given me the freedom to select from a wide range of courses covering a broad period and to discover my own equally broad research interests within that. I have also managed to grasp some basic ancient Greek vocabulary throughout the course of my studies, which may not be quite enough to read Herodotus in ancient Greek, but has certainly served me well in analysing primary literary sources in conjunction with the archaeological record.

I also believe that Classical reception can play a vital role in promoting inclusivity as it allows us to bridge the gap between the ancient world and the present day. Exploring ways in which the past has been and is appreciated and appropriated can help make it more tangible and less alien to students; it can also help to reframe the narrative which associates the discipline with those at the upper end of the social stratum who have predominantly 'owned' it. Working with Dr Alex Imrie (National Outreach Co-ordinator for the Classical Association of Scotland), I developed a series of articles in conjunction with *Retrospect Journal*, the University of Edinburgh's student-led History, Classics and Archaeological journal, which attempted to address some of the issues pertinent within the discipline today. Not only was it exciting to see the response to this series but as a non-traditional, working-class student, receiving the support to bring an idea like this to fruition was incredibly validating.

Ultimately, I think that the idea that Classics is a pursuit of the elite persists—that is, provided you have even encountered the term 'Classics' at all. That reputation is not entirely undeserved, but I do believe that a great deal is being done to challenge that position. If we remove those initial barriers to accessing undergraduate study, we may well find many more students like myself—who have the drive, the ability, and the desire to pursue study of the ancient world—are out there, and who are very much deserving of that opportunity.

Joe Watson, PhD Candidate, University of Durham

Classics is a complex home for all queer people; although it has the potential to be a safe environment for everyone at present, some people are able to feel more at home than others. I am a cis gay man who read Plato's *Symposium* as a teenager in what was a very formative experience for my conception of my own sexuality. Mine is not an unusual story: queer, white, cis men and women—inside and outside the academy—have read and worked on the Classics, uncovering *our* genealogies for decades. In 2021, most UK undergraduate Classics programmes provide the opportunity to study ancient sexualities to some extent, not least due to the richness of the Classical material which—however distantly—reflects us and our lives.

I want to stress the potential within Classics teaching and learning to extend this inclusiveness to less dominant queer voices who have become marginalised, even within Classical queer communities. In my reading of the scholarship on queer identities outside cis male and female homosexuality, I consistently encounter views that are actively toxic, intentionally or otherwise. And such scholarship, of course, plays a key role in teaching and learning on the subject. Let us take as an example the character of Iphis in Ovid's *Metamorphoses*, whom we could productively and positively describe as transmasculine, given the way his narrative plays out; even recent articles about him happily print problematic ideas and language about trans people which, if they had been written about gay men, would be recognised for their bigotry. Necessarily, teaching and learning on Iphis will follow these trends; students and their teachers will find it a hard job to push back on a tradition which is hostile to trans-centric approaches.

Classics, then, can—and should—do better by the trans and non-binary classicists existing in our discipline, whether as amateurs, students, researchers, or teachers. We should do this by thinking about the people receiving our work, both colleagues reading our research output and students sitting in our classrooms. To stick with my example, it does not really matter whether the fictional character of Iphis, in the *Metamorphoses*, did, would have or could have identified as a trans man. What matters is that trans men—and indeed, other trans people—will be engaging with any material we produce about him. Therefore, the impetus is on us, as interested academics and teachers, to educate ourselves on what is inappropriate and why. It would be almost unthinkable to teach a course on ancient homoerotics which utilised homophobic slurs; the same cannot yet be said for work on other queer identities and people.

Classics is suitable for the types of teaching and learning which are inclusive of *all* queer people; at present, we are not meeting this potential.

Claude McNaughton, Teacher, Pimlico Academy, London

At Pimlico Academy, we have seen great benefits from prioritising inclusivity in the teaching of Classics, both through results and engagement. We deliver Latin to all students at Key Stage 3, regardless of setting or prior achievement. Grammatical rigour is balanced with an exploration of cultural history through translations. Every student starts on the same material to offer an inclusive approach. They may receive adapted lesson plans and resources but ultimately work towards the same tests. This has led to very successful outcomes from all sets. We have a diverse intake at GCSE with up to 50 students in a year and many pupils from lower sets pursuing the subject and achieving fantastic results. The inclusivity of this curriculum allows all students equal opportunity.

Another success of this approach has been to remove some of the academic and social stigma which, unfortunately, is still associated with Classics. We have had success in taking our students away from purely Greek and Roman culture to different corners of the ancient world. While students still enjoy traditional topics such as the Roman theatre and dinner parties, we also look at different cultures of the period. Egyptian papyri offer the chance to explore local voices and concerns while shifting the focus away from the political elite. We also look at Ethiopian culture and India, which has allowed many to connect with their own cultural heritage. Moreover, we have great success in encouraging pupils to think about different voices that can be accessed. Year 7 pupils are asked to think about the subtext in the fables of Aesop and Phaedrus. Further along, they access different reactions to empire, such as the Persian and Bactrian response to Alexander the Great. While we feel we are in a strong position in terms of the curriculum, we are working on how best to communicate the aims to students ensuring that they understand the diversity of the ancient world rather than viewing it purely through the lens of the Western male.

As our curriculum shows, Classics is a perfect subject for encouraging inclusivity in classrooms. Beyond KS3, our A-level students have greatly enjoyed exploring aspects of queer theory in the set texts. The reversal of gender roles in Apuleius and the allusions to Catullus in *Aeneid* XI have prompted many student-led discussions where they can bring in their own experiences and understand how far back such ideas go. Furthermore, we have found that, because so much of what they learn does not take place in the West, the students feel that this history belongs to everyone. Classics is a way for students to experience not just the history of one country, but to explore the roots of culture and the human experience.

Aaron Zeleke, Year 10 Latin GCSE Student, Pimlico Academy, London

Having gone to a state secondary and primary school, it was very encouraging that Latin was taught early on. Since about Year 5 I was taught Latin and throughout secondary, it has been taught as if that's just normal which just makes it much easier to take part in especially when there is none of that stigma of how "privileged we must be" and rather it's become the norm.

My only real criticism is that it's not taught everywhere and that this stereotype that you must be rich and going to a private school to be able to do Latin is still widespread. So I would really like to see Latin become something that is common in schools nationally. Most people I meet with outside of school are surprised I do Latin and think it is unusual and just for posh people. But it is not like this in school.

Florence Heaton, Year 13 Classical Civilisation A Level Student, Runshaw College, Lancashire

Based primarily on how the subject was taught in my college, I found it to be relatively inclusive. Choosing this subject stemmed from my interest in antiquity, but I still had a few preconceptions before I started studying—since I'd never done it before—namely the idea that we would have to focus a lot on the white male history. However, when studying the art, religion, and literature, there was a fairly good balance. Specifically, in the religion topic, we were able to look into the role of women and slaves and examine the art that backs up their participation, such as at religious sites of Dodona and Delphi. Being taught by two younger female tutors was also refreshing, and throughout my two years studying Classics, I have never felt that the content has been watered down or whitewashed—with themes such as the role of women and ancient attitudes towards sexuality and relationships, which formed the context to our analysis of the *Odyssey* and the *Aeneid*.

Learning was a very different experience during my second year, but in the classroom—both physical and online—everyone has always been encouraged to offer their own ideas; to start relevant discussions about the evolving study of Classics, and debate the views of the modern scholars in relation to the ancient attitudes. One key element of the course involves incorporating those scholarly opinions into our essays, and that's possibly one area that could be expanded to be more inclusive, as it seems slightly dominated by older white men. Of course, there is a difficulty with a subject like this, as that is the demographic leading Classics, but going forward it would be great to explore a wider range of scholars and their opinions, such as more women or people of colour. It would also be interesting to look specifically at the role of ethnic groups in the ancient world, as there is so much to work with beyond the mainstream euro-centric content.

Rosie Tootell, Teacher, Runshaw College, Lancashire

A key issue faced by teachers of A Level Classical Civilisation at a college within the state sector is that the subject is not well-recognised by 'outsiders.' Prospective students, largely from state secondaries who have no prior experience in the study of Classics, do not always recognise the name of the subject and therefore do not know just how broad and inclusive Classics can be. In reality, sexuality, gender, social class, race, religion, disability, any and all of these topics can be touched upon in just one module, even one lesson, of A Level Classical Civilisation.

We had previously fallen into the trap of focusing on the aspects of Classics which are most recognisable, but which do not fully represent the scope of inclusivity that Classics can offer. We have tended to look solely to Greece and Rome, promoting the cultures of these two civilisations above all. Doing so has had the comfort of familiarity.

For a long time, it has been the main way Classics has been taught—it was the way we were taught, after all—and there have certainly been more resources available following this path. Such a limited approach, however, can have negative consequences, such as perpetuating the myth that the Greeks and Romans (and their modern European descendants) were somehow superior to others, a line of argument hijacked by the far right to bolster their claims of western, and white, superiority.

Upon reflection, it was clear that we needed to do Classics justice and break this cycle. We have therefore made several adjustments to our course in order to promote inclusivity, highly influenced by the work of Warwick University's Global History centre and of the Institute of Classical Studies—the conferences 'Towards a more Inclusive Classics' hosted by the ICS inspiring our progress. For example, we have provided an opportunity in induction week to give students a new perspective on the bustling and globalised trade network of the ancient world, of which Greece and Rome were just a part. We have incorporated activities which demonstrate that historical timelines are not as linear—or as Anglo-centric—as once thought. We have also highlighted the fact that Classics does have a darker side by showing the arguments adopted by the alt-right, in the belief that introducing students to the key issues that are faced in the subject today and raising awareness of them is one step further towards combatting them. Additionally, we continue to diversify our reading list of selected scholarship and of further reading which students can use in their extended essays. Although not exhaustive, these are just some steps towards further improving the inclusivity of our course, and this will remain an ongoing challenge.

Justine McConnell, Senior Lecturer in Comparative Literature, King's College London

Counterintuitively perhaps, one of the reasons the discipline of Classics is so well-suited to inclusive teaching and learning is directly related to its problematic history of exclusion. That the Graeco-Roman world has, at times, been co-opted for racist, sexist, and elitist purposes—and that, in some circles, this remains the case—requires our teaching to incorporate considerations of why that is the case, how it came about, and how it can be avoided in future.

Creative writers and artists have led the way in this, exploring and contesting the uses to which the discipline has been put, and highlighting damaging and distorted appropriations of the Graeco-Roman world. I take my cue from these artists, centring their receptions of antiquity in my teaching.

Twentieth- and twenty-first-century writers such as Toni Morrison, Aimé Césaire, Bernardine Evaristo, Derek Walcott, and Marlene NourbeSe Philip, to name just a few, have engaged with classical myth to explore contemporary issues, especially related to the long legacy of slavery. They engage with the Graeco-Roman world in both critical and appreciative ways, and in doing so, also offer a model for how we might teach Classics in more inclusive ways. For each of these writers sets Graeco-Roman myth within fresh comparative contexts, rejecting the elevation of the 'classical' to a position of primacy and instead putting it into a wider dialogue that lays bare the power dynamics of Classics' history of exclusivity.

In my teaching, we often begin from these modern works. Examining Ishmael Reed's satirical syncretisation of Egyptian myth with Judaeo-Christian traditions in *Mumbo Jumbo* (1972) or Zora Neale Hurston's combination of a dash of Aeschylus with Haitian myth in *Their Eyes Were Watching God* (1937), we ask why these two writers turn to antiquity in novels set in, and reflecting on, the contemporaneous US. We consider Wole Soyinka's identification of the myopia of claiming roots in Greek drama for Yoruba tragedy, even while he has explicitly engaged with ancient Greek literature in *The Bacchae of Euripides: A Communion Rite* (1973). And we contrast Soyinka's stance with that of Ralph Ellison, who asserted his identification with Odysseus as much as with Brer Rabbit, as we see in *Invisible Man* (1952).

This focus on writers who have historically been omitted from the study of Classics, both because they are modern and because, as writers of colour, their work has been marginalised, begins to break down some of the barriers of exclusion surrounding the discipline. Their comparative approach allows students to see that, even before they have gained expertise in the Graeco-Roman world, their existing knowledge stands them in excellent stead and the impression of Classics as the preserve of only certain people is a pernicious mirage.

Notes

1 See https://classicalassociation.org/conference/ca-online-conference-2021-videos/. The panel began with five three-minute 'spotlight talks.' These consisted of: Lauren Canham on 'Ancient Paradigms of Disability on the Curriculum'; Hardeep Dhindsa on 'Chromophobia: Recolouring the Classics'; Victoria Leonard on 'Caring and the Classics'; Joe Watson on 'Queer Classics and Classics for Queers; or, Beyond Gay Men Reading Plato'; Bobby Xinyue on 'Race, Inclusivity, and the Future

of Classics.' These talks were followed by a conversation among Tristan Craig (student, University of Edinburgh), Florence Heaton (student, Runshaw College), Justine McConnell (Senior Lecturer, King's College London), Claude McNaughton (teacher, Pimlico Academy), Rosie Tootell (teacher, Runshaw College), and Aaron Zeleke (student, Pimlico Academy). The panel closed with a series of short reflective comments by Amy Coker (Cheltenham Ladies' College and University of Bristol), Katherine Harloe (University of Reading), Arlene Holmes-Henderson (King's College London), Neville Morley (University of Exeter), Isabel Ruffell (University of Glasgow), and Tim Whitmarsh (University of Cambridge). The contributions published here represent all parts of the panel and a range of approaches. The affiliations and positions listed are those of the contributors at the time of the CA panel in 2021.

2 2020: https://ics.sas.ac.uk/events/towards-more-inclusive-classics and https://cucd.blogs.sas.ac.uk/files/2020/09/GOFF-AND-PETSALIS-DIOMIDIS-Inclusive-Classics-Report.pdf. 2021: https://ics.sas.ac.uk/events/towards-more-inclusive-classics-ii and https://cucd.blogs.sas.ac.uk/files/2021/12/Inclusive-Classics-II-report.pdf. Planned events: (1) Panel on 'Neurodiversity and Classics,' CA annual conference 2022 (2) International online workshop 2023, 'Towards a more Inclusive Classics III: Material Culture.'

3 In 2020, we requested pre-circulated materials to be posted on the ICS website, in order to be more inclusive to varied learning modes and disabilities (such as visual or hearing impairments); these materials were then summarised in short oral presentations at the workshops and far more time was given over to discussion. For our second international online workshop, we held themed break-out rooms and project updates as well as more traditional presentations and roundtables.

11 Embedding Diversity in Classics Teachers' Training

A Case Study at a Greek University

Marisa Fountopoulou and Effrosyni Kostara[1]

Introduction

The enhancement of diversity and inclusivity has in recent years become one of the basic aims of almost all learning curricula for schools and higher education institutions. Of the 17 Sustainable Development Goals included in the UNESCO 2030 Agenda for Sustainable Development (2016), 'gender equality' and 'quality education' are the ones that could be potentially achieved through educational policies. Towards this goal, educational systems need to be adjusted to better respond to learners' diversities, unique characteristics, and needs.

With this aim in mind, it has become crucial that teacher training programmes, as well as curricula and textbooks, are free from any form of gender stereotyping and discrimination and instead promote equality and human rights. With regard to topics related to classical antiquity (Classics, Ancient History, etc.; henceforth 'Classics'), it is imperative that Classics teachers be appropriately and systematically trained in an inclusive and diversified mode of understanding and teaching, especially when they have to deal with sensitive and controversial subjects (Macewen 2003; Ball and Tyson 2011; Deacy and McHardy 2012; Hunt 2016). Classical texts abound with issues relating to gender roles, immigration, slavery, sexuality, and identity and thus easily encourage reflection and a holistic approach to diversity and inclusivity. The present chapter proposes a teaching methodology suitable for all Classics teachers who wish to adopt a pedagogically informed approach to the teaching of Classics.

The Four Dimensions of a Text

The fundamental idea of the proposed methodology is the critical exploitation of a text through 'Four Basic Dimensions.' We believe that a text must be approached holistically, rather than one-sidedly

DOI: 10.4324/9781003278016-12

as a piece of literature or a morphological and linguistic expression. To this end, the text is considered through four 'dimensions': 1) context, 2) content, 3) form, and 4) relation to the present day (i.e., where the past and the present meet) (Institute of Educational Policy 2021). Aspects of each dimension are briefly described below, as they relate to the teaching activity under discussion here. In the proposed methodology, the teacher will use questions and activities relating to the chosen issue or topic (e.g., gender equality) that emerge by focusing on each dimension and its aspects. Additionally, the use of these questions and activities will offer pupils the opportunity to develop their critical awareness on the issues discussed (i.e., Lawall 2001; Johnson and Freedman 2005).

The first dimension, **context**, relates to the genre of the text and its inherent characteristics, e.g., the historical and political circumstances in which the text was written. Questions can be based on observations on the text and may highlight words or phrases that corroborate them. Two examples are:

a Identify references that confirm that this text is biographical and not historical. (Plut. *Alex.* 1.1–1.2)
b Describe the zeitgeist of the period when this tragedy was written and suggest how this has affected its content. (Eur. *Tro.*, prologue)

The second dimension, **content**, refers to the pragmatics of the text, i.e., its cultural, ethical, ideological, and aesthetic characteristics, as well as to its internal cohesion and consistency. Pupils will observe and note in-text references to these aspects and will be asked to answer critical questions or participate in activities that promote reflection on these elements. Indicative questions could be:

a Highlight ideas and references associated with women's roles in the society described. Would any of these ideas survive in modern societies? (Hom. *Od.* 23.1–84)
b How would you describe Hector? Is he a hero? Do we define heroes in the same way nowadays? (Hom. *Il.* 6.390–512)

The third dimension, **form**, is most applicable when a text is taught in its original language. It refers to a text's linguistic expression, including word choice and meaning, as well as to aspects of morphology and syntax. Questions and activities should focus on the enhancement of pupils' linguistic skills. In addition, pupils can develop various cognitive functions of thinking, including comparison, classification, distinction, hypothesis, and reasoning (Fountopoulou, 2006; Kostara, 2022). Questions might be along the lines of the following:

a Define the term 'barbarian.' Is the term still used today and, if yes, in what context? (Eur. *Hel*. 270–275)
b Which adjectives are used to characterise Hecuba? Would you use these adjectives for a modern-day Hecuba? (Eur. *Tro*. 98–122)

Finally, the fourth dimension, **where the past and present meet**, refers to the linguistic and visual rendering of a text and its modern reception. This dimension is particularly effective for pupils' development of contemporary forms of literacies, e.g., digital, socio-cultural, and critical. They are asked to consider multiple sources, to create their own material, and to reflect on their own assumptions, actions, and lives. Potential questions are:

a Search museum or gallery databases for visual representations of your favourite story in *The Aeneid*. What aspects of the story have most influenced its reception by artists?
b Recreate your favourite Labour of Hercules in your preferred medium: a poem, a physical creation, a drawing, etc.

A Case Study at a University in Greece

In a case study at the National and Kapodistrian University of Athens (Greece), conducted in December 2021, the proposed methodology was adjusted to take account of the issue of immigration in the training of Classics teachers.

The Framework

The proposed approach to textual material was approved by the Institute of Educational Policy in Greece in October 2021 and is now included in the curriculum of the course 'Ancient Greek Language and Literature.' This course is taught to secondary education pupils aged 13–15 years. Promoting diversity is among the basic goals of the new curriculum, specifically the enhancement of pupils' awareness of the issues of peace, freedom, equality, democracy, acceptance of the differences, and respect for human rights.

To teach Classics, teachers should hold an undergraduate degree in Greek Philology, which is a four-year course in the Greek higher education system. During this degree programme, students are trained to approach texts pedagogically in order to achieve a curriculum's learning goals.

The Training

Twenty-five students, all future Classics teachers, participated in the training, which forms part of the seventh-semester course 'Teaching of Ancient Greek Language and Literature.' It includes the study of theories associated with teaching ancient languages, the design and implementation of lessons on teaching ancient Greek, and the occasional visit to schools to observe experienced teachers.

The training lasted approximately six hours, over three sessions. Its goal was primarily to help trainee teachers understand what the new curriculum entails regarding the elaboration of texts, but it also aimed to engage them in creating activities and following the proposed methodology and to enable them to promote diversity and address issues relating to immigration in their teaching.

Structure

The new methodology was applied to Euripides' *The Trojan Women*, a Greek tragedy that will be studied in Year 3 of secondary school in Greece.

During the first session, the students were informed about the content of the new curriculum. The four dimensions of the text were introduced and thoroughly discussed. Following this, the students proposed activities that would be applicable to each dimension. They were also informed about the authors' intention to apply the proposed methodology to a specific issue, namely immigration.

The second session focused on the text itself. Participants were asked to read aloud a number of extracts (see below) and to discuss them in small groups, focusing on their feelings, first thoughts, and possible connections to reality, while keeping in mind the issue of diversity. They were also asked to focus on specific critical questions, e.g., how would you advise Hecuba to cope with her new reality? How do you think Hecuba's identity as a queen affects her reactions to this new reality? How responsible do you think she is for her current situation? Do you believe that our own social status affects the way we face difficulties in our life? Each group was then asked to share their ideas with the whole team.

During the third and final session, the same small groups were asked to produce questions and activities for each dimension of the text, formulated in such a way that the issues of diversity in general, and immigration in particular, would be constantly highlighted. The students were given passages from Euripides' *The Trojan Women*,[2] both in the original ancient Greek and in translation. This was followed by a general reflection on the training.

Data Collection

Indicative questions that were created by the students are presented below, followed by brief descriptions as to why they are suitable for a particular dimension and how they are associated with the issue of immigration. Three passages were provided to the students for three different lessons.

Lesson 1

ἄνα, δύσδαιμον· πεδόθεν κεφαλὴν ἐπάειρε δέρην <τ'>· οὐκέτι Τροία τάδε καὶ βασιλῆς ἐσμεν Τροίας.	100	Up, unhappy woman! Raise your head and neck from the ground! This is no longer Troy you see, and we are no longer Troy's rulers.
μεταβαλλομένου δαίμονος ἄνσχου. πλεῖ κατὰ πορθμόν, πλεῖ κατὰ δαίμονα, μηδὲ προσίστη πρῷραν βιότου πρὸς κῦμα πλέουσα τύχαισιν.		As your fortune changes, endure the change! Sail with the current in the strait, sail with your fortune, and do not turn the prow of your life to face disasters, sailing toward their oncoming wave!
αἰαῖ αἰαῖ. τί γὰρ οὐ πάρα μοι μελέᾳ στενάχειν ᾗ πατρὶς ἔρρει καὶ τέκνα καὶ πόσις; ὦ πολὺς ὄγκος συστελλόμενος προγόνων, ὡς οὐδὲν ἄρ' ἦσθα.	105	Ah me, ah me! What lament is there that I cannot utter, unlucky woman that I am? My country is gone, my children, my husband! Great pride of my ancestors, now cut short, how slight a thing you were after all!
τί με χρὴ σιγᾶν, τί δὲ μὴ σιγᾶν; [τί δὲ θρηνῆσαι;]	110	What should I wrap in silence, what should I not wrap in silence? [What should I lament?]
δύστηνος ἐγὼ τῆς βαρυδαίμονος ἄρθρων κλίσεως, ὡς διάκειμαι, νῶτ' ἐν στερροῖς λέκτροισι ταθεῖσ'.		How luckless I am, how miserably does my body recline, my back stretched out on its hard bed!
οἴμοι κεφαλῆς, οἴμοι κροτάφων πλευρῶν θ', ὥς μοι πόθος εἱλίξαι καὶ διαδοῦναι νῶτον ἄκανθάν τ' εἰς ἀμφοτέρους τοίχους μελέων, ἐπιοῦσ' αἰεὶ δακρύων ἐλέγους.	115	Alas for the temples of my head and for my sides! How I long to roll my back and spine about, listing now to this side of my body, now to that as I utter continually my tearful song of woe!
μοῦσα δὲ χαὔτη τοῖς δυστήνοις ἄτας κελαδεῖν ἀχορεύτους.	120	This too is music for those in misfortune, to utter aloud their joyless troubles.

Questions:

1 *The Trojan Women* was first performed in 415 B.C. The story is thought to be connected to events that took place on the island

of Melos. Research, then briefly describe this historical event and connect it to Euripides's play. **Context**

Comments: The pupils should refer to the fact that Melos was forced into an unconditional surrender to Athens. Adult males were executed, while women and children were sold as slaves (Goff, 2013). By discussing these events, the pupils are expected to reflect on the consequences of war, which include slavery, immigration, and violence, the same atrocities faced by modern victims of war, who are often rejected and feel marginalised in their host countries.

2 Hecuba refers to herself as 'unhappy,' 'unlucky,' 'luckless,' and cries 'Ah me! Ah me!'.

   a How are Hecuba's words expressed in the original text? Are any of these words used in everyday language? **Form**

   b Try to connect the words and phrases to the lives of modern immigrants. Do you think they would use the same words? **Content**

Comments: The question on form mostly concerns pupils who study ancient Greek, or those who have some understanding of it and can identify the words δύσδαιμον, μελέᾳ, and δύστηνος. It will help them focus on the way Hecuba characterises herself and expresses her feelings as an enslaved and immigrant woman. In relation to content, the pupils are motivated to contemplate whether and how the feelings and misery expressed by Hecuba convey the feelings of any immigrant, both then and now.

3 Hecuba says 'As your fortune changes, endure the change!', 'We are no longer Troy's rulers,' and 'My country is gone, my children, my husband!'.

   a How are Hecuba's words expressed in the original text? **Form**

   b What do you think about what Hecuba has to face? **Content**

   c How would you associate these phrases with the lives of modern immigrants and with your own? **Past and present**

Comments: Regarding form, pupils should identify the phrase μεταβαλλομένου δαίμονος ἀνέχου. The question on content will help pupils focus on one of the timeless ideas that Hecuba expresses, namely the fickle and unstable character of fortune. Hecuba is facing a new reality: she has lost everything, including her family, home, and even identity. She feels lost; she has to live enslaved. The past and present meet when the pupils are motivated to relate to Hecuba's situation and realise that her feelings and agonies represent those of all immigrants.

4 Rewrite the passage as if the action took place today. What would you change and what would you keep? **Past and Present**
Comments: *This question helps pupils become more creative and produce original material. With the help of the teachers, they might realise that the new story will be mostly identical to the original, apart from (probably) names and places. The feelings and experiences described are common for all immigrants, both then and now.*

Lesson 2

δούλα δ᾽ ἄγομαι γραῦς ἐξ οἴκων	140	I am taken away as an aged slave from
πενθήρη κρᾶτ᾽ ἐκπορθηθεῖσ᾽		my house,
οἰκτρῶς. ἀλλ᾽ ὦ		my head ravaged in grief
τῶν χαλκεγχέων Τρώων ἄλοχοι		pitiably! But, O
μέλεαι, κοῦραι δύσνυμφοι,		unhappy wives of the Trojans with
τύφεται Ἴλιον, αἰάζωμεν.	145	swords of bronze,
		women unblest in your husbands,
		Ilium is burning: let us wail aloud!
μάτηρ δ᾽ ὡσεί τις πτανοῖς,		Like a mother bird to her winged
κλαγγὰν ἐξάρξω γὼ μολπάν,		brood,
		I lead off the song of lamentation,
οὐ τὰν αὐτὰν οἵαν ποτὲ δὴ		not at all the same song
σκήπτρῳ Πριάμου διερειδομένου	150	that I led off, as Priam leaned upon his scepter,
ποδὸς ἀρχεχόρου πλαγαῖς Φρυγίους		with the confident beat of chorus
εὐκόμποις ἐξῆρχον θεούς.		leader's foot
		in praise of Troy's gods.

Questions:

1 Tragedy as a genre has the power to present and give voice to the 'other.' How is 'otherness' presented in this passage? **Context**
 Comments: *This question focuses on the power of tragedy to make voices of 'otherness' heard* (Croally, 2005). *In the passage, the voice of an enslaved immigrant woman is presented, as are the new realities that immigrants face, including their fears and the obstacles they may face on their journeys. These can be associated with the difficulties faced by modern immigrants and can highlight how immigration is a timeless phenomenon.*

2 Hecuba says 'I am taken away as an aged slave from my house.'
 a How are Hecuba's words expressed in the original text? Are any of these words used in everyday language? **Form**
 b What are the key words of this phrase and what effect do they have on Hecuba's audience? **Content**

 Comments: *With regard to form, pupils who study ancient Greek should identify the words δούλα, γραῦς, and οἴκων. With regard to* content, they should focus on the expressions 'slave,' 'house,' and 'aged': the question should help them focus on the way in which Hecuba expresses her feelings as an enslaved, old, immigrant woman who loses everything.

   c Find (online) interviews with modern immigrants that describe their present and past experiences and status. Present their stories to your classmates and discuss whether these people would be treated differently if they had the opportunity to talk about their past in their host country. **Past and Present**

Comments: For both content and its relatability, pupils will focus on immigrants' identity struggles. We tend to forget that they often led normal and peaceful lives before finding themselves in their current situations. For instance, Hecuba was queen of Troy but she will now be responsible for the children of her enemies. Similarly, modern immigrants are often stereotyped and their previous lives or experiences are often completely disregarded.

3 Watch the theatrical performance of *The Trojan Women* in Delphi in 2018, directed by Theodoros Terzopoulos and available online via the Onassis Foundation. Six languages were used during this staging. What do you think of this choice? How did you feel after watching it? Would you like to share any thoughts? **Past and Present**

Comments: This question aims to familiarise pupils with using digital material in the study of Classics, to make them engage with the play's modern reception, and to encourage them to discuss the fact that the use of six different languages expresses the potential situation of many people, whether immigrant or enslaved.

Lesson 3

ἐᾶτέ μ' (οὔτοι φίλα τὰ μὴ φίλ , ὦ κόραι) κεῖσθαι πεσοῦσαν· πτωμάτων γὰρ ἄξια πάσχω τε καὶ πέπονθα κἄτι πείσομαι. ὦ θεοί· κακοὺς μὲν ἀνακαλῶ τοὺς συμμάχους, ὅμως δ' ἔχει τι σχῆμα κικλήσκειν θεούς, ὅταν τις ἡμῶν δυστυχῆ λάβῃ τύχην. 470	Let me lie where I have fallen (for unwelcome help is not kindness, my daughters). Collapse is the proper response to what I have suffered, am suffering, and will suffer. O gods! To be sure, I am calling on allies that are faithless.
πρῶτον μὲν οὖν μοι τἀγάθ' ἐξᾆσαι φίλον· τοῖς γὰρ κακοῖσι πλείον' οἶκτον ἐμβαλῶ.	Yet nonetheless it is proper to invoke them when we suffer misfortune. My desire therefore is first to sing of my blessings. For in this way, I shall make my woes seem the more to be pitied.

(Continued)

ἣ μὲν τύραννος κἀς τύρανν' ἐγημάμην,		I was of royal blood and
κἀνταῦθ' ἀριστεύοντ' ἐγεινάμην τέκνα,	475	married into a royal house.
οὐκ ἀριθμὸν ἄλλως ἀλλ' ὑπερτάτους Φρυγῶν·		There I gave birth to children
οὐ τοιάδ' οὔθ' Ἑλληνὶς οὐδὲ βάρβαρος		of great excellence, no mere
γυνὴ τεκοῦσα κομπάσειεν ἄν ποτε.		ciphers but preeminent among the Phrygians. No woman, Greek nor yet barbarian, could boast that she gave birth to their like.

Questions:

1 'No woman, Greek nor yet barbarian, could boast that she gave birth to their like': who was characterised as 'barbarian' by the ancient Greeks? Would they characterise the Trojans as such?[3] If yes, how do you explain Hecuba's decision to refer to Trojans and barbarians separately? **Context; Content**

2 'Collapse is the proper response to what I have suffered, am suffering, and will suffer': how is this phrase expressed in the original text? What is the verb used and in which forms? **Form; Content**
Comments: Students will observe that Hecuba uses the verb 'suffer' in three different tenses, namely present (πάσχω), past (πέπονθα), and future (πείσομαι). The question helps pupils to understand that the unhappiness and misfortune of immigrants is constant, especially when they are enslaved and of older age.

3 Read (online) Plutarch, *De Alexandri magni fortuna aut virtute* 1.6. How does Alexander the Great behave towards the 'other'? How does this compare with our own behaviour towards people we consider 'different'? **Content; Past and Present**
Comments: This passage should inspire a comparison between the two perspectives used, namely that of the conqueror in Plutarch and that of the conquered in Euripides. The pupils will be able to review how a renowned conqueror treated conquered peoples with respect, despite their different cultures and customs. They will also be able to discuss the cultural diversity of the modern world.

Conclusions

Although the participants had never worked with our proposed methodology, they successfully produced questions relating to the issue of immigration for each of the dimensions. Each participant found this to be a challenging task, but they concluded that it could be achieved if the relevant literature was carefully studied.

Moreover, all students agreed that the whole approach could prove useful for the teaching of Classics both in Greece and abroad, as, in any case, the text should always be the basis for teaching. As a result, whether focusing on a specific issue or not, this four-dimensional approach to texts, along with the development of suitable types of questions, could offer a pedagogical basis for designing Classics lessons in schools or higher education institutions.

Finally, some of the students noted that this text-centric methodology could also be beneficial to multicultural learning teams, as focusing on the ancient text ensures an objective and safe environment in which to express their feelings and views.

Notes

1 Professor Marisa Fountopoulou was the head of the team that created the new curriculum for the course 'Ancient Greek Language and Literature.' Dr Effrosyni Kostara was a member of the team.
2 The text of *Trojan Women* follows the edition of Loeb Classical Library. The translation is by Kovacs (1999).
3 For this question, see Goff (2013).

Works Cited

Ball, A.F. and Tyson, C.A. (2011) 'Preparing Teachers for Diversity in the Twenty-First Century', in A.F. Ball and A. Tyson (eds.), *Studying Diversity in Teacher Education*, Plymouth, 399–416.

Croally, N. (2005) 'Tragedy's Teaching', in J. Gregory (ed.), *A Companion to Greek Tragedy*, Malden, 55–69.

Deacy, S. and McHardy, F. (2012) 'Teaching Sensitive Subjects in the Classical Classroom: Challenges, Advice and Strategies', *CUCD Bulletin* 41: 28–31.

Fountopoulou, M. (2006) 'Learning Principles and the Cultivation of Critical Thinking: Application in the Course "Ancient Greek"', http://www.elliepek.gr/documents/3o_synedrio_eisigiseis/fountopoulou.pdf (accessed 17 May, 22). [In Greek]

Goff, B. (2013) *Euripides: Trojan Women*, London.

Hunt, S. (2016) 'Teaching Sensitive Topics in the Secondary Classics Classroom', *Journal of Classics Teaching* 17.34: 31–43.

Institute of Educational Policy (2021) *Curriculum for the 'Ancient Greek Language and Literature' Course for Years 1–3 of Secondary School*, Athens. [In Greek]

Johnson, H., and Freedman, L. (2005). *Developing Critical Awareness at the Middle Level. Using Texts as Tools for Critique and Pleasure*, Newark, NJ.

Kostara, E. (2022) *Critical Thinking in Teaching Practice: An Application in the Ancient Greek Language and Literature Course*, Ioannina.

Kovacs, D. (1999). *Trojan Women; Iphigenia Among the Taurians; Ion*, Cambridge, MA.

Lawall, M. (2001) 'Some Implications of Research in Education for Teaching Classics', *The Classical Outlook* 78.4: 157–63.
Macewen, S. (2003) 'Using Diversity to Teach Classics', *The Classical World* 96.4: 416–20.
UNESCO (2016). Education 2030: Incheon Declaration and Framework for Action for the Implementation of Sustainable Development Goal 4: Ensure Inclusive and Equitable Quality Education and Promote Lifelong Learning Opportunities for All. Available at: https://unesdoc.unesco.org/ark:/48223/pf0000245656 (accessed 10 May 22).

Index

ableism 73, 105
abuse 78–79, 81, 111; in antiquity 52, 57
accessibility 25, 69n24, 100–109
accomplices 32–33
Aeschylus 65, 69n17, 129
Africana Studies 21
Ahmed, Sara 96
allyship 28, 30, 32–33
ancient Egypt 12, 21, 63–64, 90, 122
ancient Greek (language studies) 18, 39, 62–63, 89, 123, 133–139; and elitism 91
ancient history 17, 25, 38, 131; and exclusion 27
anti-colonialism 32, 88
anti-semitism 79
antiracism 32, 36–46; *see also* racism
Apuleius 65, 126
Arachne 111, 118
Arbery, Ahmaud 25
Archaeology 1, 25–35
Aristophanes 40
Aristotle 9, 65
assessment: inclusive 28; innovative 101–102
Asterion 5n3
audio description 103–104, 106–108

barriers to access 25, 28–29, 104, 124, 129
Bausch, Pina 40
Beard, Mary 79
Bell, Derrick 3
belonging 61, 64, 91, 117
Bernal, Martin 90

bias 6n19, 32, 56, 59n12, 72–87; institutional 32; training 94–95
bigotry 124
Black Classicism 17
Black Lives Matter 25, 27, 32, 81, 118
Black Trowel Collective 29
Braille 105–106
British Museum 103, 105, 108
Byzantine Studies 92

Caesar, Julius 51–52, 88–89, 97
Catullus 50, 126
Cicero 47–60, 64
Classical Reception Studies 16–17, 37, 95, 121–123; in action 113, 119
classism 73
colonialism 58n2, 65–66, 83n24, 88; *see* anti-colonialism
colonists: Roman 48, 53–55, 57, 59n17
court: in Rome 47, 54–55, 57
Crenshaw, Kimberlé 3–4
critical race theory 2–4, 36, 42, 43, 56, 59n19
cultural competence 31

death 40–41, 115; of Classics departments 20–21; threats of 36
Demosthenes 65, 66
disability 1, 2, 4, 5, 6n6, 32, 100–109, 127, 130n3
Disability Discrimination Act 100, 102–104
disciplinarity 16, 21n4
discrimination 26, 32, 62, 72–78, 81, 82n2, 95, 102–104, 131

emotional labour 80, 82n18
employability 65
Eos Africana 94
equality 75, 81, 83n25, 95–96, 102–104, 131–133
eurocentrism 88, 127
Euripides 65, 68n2, 89, 134–139
Eurydice 40–41, 110–120
exclusion 2, 27, 61, 66, 67, 81, 128, 129
exploitation: of resources 48, 52, 55

Floyd, George 25, 41
Fonteius, Marcus 47–60

Gauls 47–59, 65
gender pay gap 74, 83n19
Georgetown University 10, 18–20
Gopal, Priyamvada 79

harassment 26–27, 40, 81; reporting of 32
Harloe, Katherine 72, 80, 130n1
health 32, 95; *see also* mental health
Hecataeus of Miletus 49
Hecuba 132–139
Hercules 133
Herodotus 123
Hesiod 92
Hesperides 94
Hippocrates 64
Historically Black Colleges and Universities (HBCUs) 11, 14, 20, 21n2, 22n11, 22n14
Homer 40, 91, 92, 127, 132
Horace 89
Howard University 9–14
Hucks, Bet 31–32
human rights 65, 103–104, 131, 133

immigration 64–66, 69n12, 88, 131, 133–137, 139
imperialism 58n2, 62, 65, 89
inclusion 25, 28, 43, 61, 66–67, 75, 81, 110
inclusivity 1, 6n19, 28, 36, 65, 75, 95, 121, 123, 125–128, 131
inequality 3, 56, 81; of access to education 1, 4, 25
intersectionality 92
intolerance 62

Io 111
Iphis 124–125
Ishiguro, Kazuo 63

James, C.L.R. 88–91, 96–97
Juvenal 64, 69n13

Kush 21

Latin (language studies) 17, 18, 20, 62–63, 89, 125, 126; and elitism 91
Lee, Spike 39, 40
Lerner, Gerda 75
Liberal Arts 17, 20; colleges 15–16; mission 10, 15
Livy 65
London Classicists of Colour 5n3, 29, 97n24

marginalisation 73, 75, 81, 103, 113, 122, 136; marginalised voices 121, 124, 129
masking 101, 104
McDade, Tony 41
mental health 1, 110
mentoring 17, 28, 42, 82–83n18, 118–119
metics 62, 68n2
misogyny 40, 78–80
Morley, Edith 72, 82n2
Morrison, Toni 9, 13, 129
Mountaintop Coalition 5n3
mythology 17, 105, 110–120

Network for Working Class Classicists 5n3

omni-localism 10
oppression 2, 39, 55, 81, 118
Orpheus 40–41, 111, 113, 116
Otele, Olivette 72–73
Ovid 40, 110, 114, 119n2, 123, 124

Padilla Peralta, Dan-el 44n1, 94–95, 96
Pandey, Nandini 44n1, 96
papyri: Egyptian 125
Parthenon marbles 40, 104–107
Persephone 111
Plato 9, 14, 124
Plutarch 132, 139

prejudice 69n13
privilege 32–33, 94
Purdue University 10, 15–18

race and ethnicity 5, 6n16, 28, 36, 39, 47, 58n6, 64, 94
racism 2–3, 27, 36, 73, 78–80, 91; 'reverse racism' 94–95; see also antiracism
'reasonable adjustments' 102–104
recruitment 28, 30–31
religion: study of 2, 4, 61, 127

Septimius Severus 66
sexism 2, 73, 75, 78
sexual assault 40, 85n67
sexuality 1, 4, 6n16, 113, 124, 127, 131
sign language 104–106
silence 112–113, 115–117, 135
slavery: as a consequence of war 136; in Greco-Roman societies 62, 65, 96, 127, 131; legacy of 129; and old age 137–139; in the U.S. 3, 11, 12, 15, 19
'small teaching' 15, 17
Snowden, Frank M. Jr. 9, 12, 21n1
social justice 32, 66
Sportula, the 5n3, 29
stereotypes 48–49, 55
stigma: of Classics 125, 126; of disability 101, 104

Subsaharan Africa 21
Suetonius 123
systemic injustices 4, 25

Tacitus 58n6
Tarrant, Dorothy 76, 80
Taylor, Breonna 25, 41
technology 13, 14, 17, 67, 102
Thucydides 66, 89
trauma 40, 50, 57, 110

Varro 96
Virgil 50, 89, 127, 133
violence 48, 51, 54, 63, 122, 136; institutional 77; intimate partner 85n67; against women 78, 84n47

Wake Forest University 36–38, 42–44, 45n6–7
Walcott, Derek 89, 129
Walker, Alice 65
war 4, 40, 50, 51, 54, 58n10, 63, 136; crimes 66; see also trauma
West, Cornel 9, 18
white supremacy 36, 39, 44
Wikipedia 75–85
women's rights 66
working-class students 29, 124

Zuckerberg, Donna 43, 79

For Product Safety Concerns and Information please contact our EU representative GPSR@taylorandfrancis.com
Taylor & Francis Verlag GmbH, Kaufingerstraße 24, 80331 München, Germany

www.ingramcontent.com/pod-product-compliance
Lightning Source LLC
Chambersburg PA
CBHW051750230426
43670CB00012B/2224